Jean

# small**garden**

For Dorling Kindersley
*Managing Editor*  Anna Kruger
*Managing Art Editor*  Alison Donovan
*DTP Designer*  Louise Waller
*Production Controller*  Mandy Innes
*Picture Research*  Melanie Watson
*Consultant Editor*  David Lamb

Produced for Dorling Kindersley by
The Bridgewater Book Co Ltd
*Art Director*  Michael Whitehead
*Editorial Director*  Robert Yarham
*Designer*  Andrew Milne

*US Editor*  Christine Heilman
First American Edition, 2006

Published in the United States by
DK Publishing, Inc.
375 Hudson Street
New York, New York 10014

06 07 08 09 10  10 9 8 7 6 5 4 3 2

A Cataloging-in-Publication record for this book is
available from the Library of Congress.

ISBN 0-7566-1723-5

Color reproduction by Colourscan, Singapore
Printed and bound by Star Standard, Singapore

Discover more at
**www.dk.com**

John Brookes

# small**garden**

4

CONTENTS

# Foreword

There has been an explosion of interest in garden design since 1989, when *The New Small Garden*, on which this book is based, was first published. The number of garden designers has increased dramatically and there are more ideas shown for what might be achieved in the garden than ever, fed by the media and by exhibition work all over the world. I believe that my own work on the "room outside" has been instrumental. It's all very exciting as interest in design outside breaks away from interest in horticulture.

Although styles have changed and uses of materials developed, I am pleased to say that much of what I suggested in 1989 is still useful today. While it's been hugely enjoyable to review, select, and present new examples and illustrations, people are still the common denominator when designing a garden—the space they need and how they move around in it. We may have developed more minimal visual tastes, and our pool of ideas may have deepened with travel; we may prefer a less "planty" look and we probably have better ideas for creating impact; but the rules for making the best of your small space are the same. I hope *Small Garden* helps you to do just that.

John Brookes MBE

**My view out** Spring planting in a small gravelled area alongside my own kitchen terrace.

# living
# rooms

If you have an outside space, however small, in town, suburb, or country, employing design and style can transform it for your use and delight.

**Small terrace garden** (right) A really simple and functional design layout for a small terrace garden. Forms and shapes all work together to create a comfortable ambiance.

# Introduction

Space is a precious commodity, so limited and expensive in towns and cities that it makes sense to enjoy every inch you have. Using outside space—be it a window ledge, roof, balcony, or basement courtyard—is an enjoyable, and possibly stylish, way of extending the boundaries of your home.

For many, the word "garden" conjures up images of lawns and herbaceous borders, soil and pruning shears, mulches and manures, and the niceties of horticultural technique. When presented with a tiny space, we all too often cram in all the traditional elements of a big garden, reduced in scale.

In order to make the most of a small space, it is necessary to break free from preconceptions about the nature of a garden: where it should be and the things it should, or should not, contain. Gardens, first and foremost, are for people, not plants.

All sorts of design elements and techniques can be combined to produce a stimulating effect; planting is just one of these. Your garden might contain sculpture, some water, and a minimum of planting—lit at night, the effect can be quite magical. Conversely, there can be an enormous attraction in creating a dense jungle in a tiny urban space, which not only softens the general ambiance but provides therapy in its husbandry.

The key to realizing the potential of your small space, in both visual and practical terms, is design—this involves planning and styling your space so that it suits your way of life, as well as the character of your home and its surroundings.

"Space is a precious commodity... it makes sense to enjoy every inch"

**Evening paradise** (right) This garden comes into its own in hotter climates in the evenings, when the sound of water can be cooling at the end of the day, and where, as it gets darker, subtle lighting comes into play.

**Year-round enjoyment**
Opening or sliding windows in a temperate climate allow the owners to enjoy their garden space at all times of the year.

# Room outside

The importance of having even a small space outside, or just a visual link with nature, cannot be overestimated. A small garden, be it a balcony, roof, or terrace, is a sanctuary where you can escape the pressures of an urban existence. Think of your space as an extension of your home, as an outside room where you can eat, read, admire a view, or watch your children play. The key to creating a sympathetic backdrop to outside living is to ask yourself first and foremost how you want to use your "room" and then, with this clear objective in mind, to set about making it a pleasant place in which to be.

It is obviously easier to create a congenial outside room in Mediterranean or tropical climates, but capturing and enjoying every minute of light and warmth in more northerly climes has its own special satisfaction. However, sun alone does not make for a comfortable outside space. There are many ways it can be made inviting. Wind and drafts can be minimized, ugly views concealed, privacy created, and color used to make it tempting even when the sun is not shining.

**Relaxation** (bottom left)
A garden pavilion with a fireplace creates a pleasant linear arrangement in which to relax.

**Party space** (below)
And why not a bar in the garden for partying, as well?

"Think of your **space** as an **extension** of your home"

"Neither the **garden** nor the **house** can afford to work in isolation"

# Enjoying your garden from inside

Having concentrated your efforts into making use of your outside space in summer, don't let it be wasted when you are inside or during the remainder of the year. Make sure your outside works visually from inside your home. Consider what it will look like from a window (not just when the sun is out), across the kitchen sink, down the hallway, or from your favorite living-room chair.

## Small-space design

Thinking of your garden as a room also makes the concept of garden planning more approachable, for on a small scale, its principles are very similar to those of interior design. Decide what you want in your space and keep the design bold and simple. Where space is at a premium, the style and design of neither the garden nor the house can afford to work in isolation from one another. If they are complementary, restricted living space inside will benefit from the view of the garden outside, and conversely, a cramped garden will seem less so if it is a harmonious extension of the building it adjoins.

**Deck seat** (far left)
You sit on the edge of the deck to use one side of the table when eating out at this property.

**Dining space** (below)
Decking provides the flooring to this small dining space, which you look down on from the house. Surrounding vegetation creates a nice sense of privacy.

**Asian mood** (left)
Would I like Big Brother watching me as I eat? He certainly creates an Asian mood, and would be an eye-catcher from inside the house.

# Linking in with out

So how do you go about establishing a harmonious link between inside and outside? Think first in terms of interlocking the spaces of the garden with the spaces of the room that adjoins it to create a flow between in and out. If you can also keep spaces in scale with one another, you will be much of the way toward the desired effect. How you style the outside space can then be used to strengthen this link. For most people, the design of the garden comes after deciding on interior style, so it is best to start by looking from the inside out.

**Spatial flow** (right)
Opening doors allow easy access into the garden and allow one space to flow into another.

**Glass house** (below)
A dining table within a glass cube creates the effect of being outside.

"Create a flow
between in and out"

## What style?

Ask yourself some questions. Is the decoration in the room you are standing in period or contemporary? If contemporary, is it minimalist timber and glass, or is it of natural materials? Once you have analyzed the interior, look into your garden and start to think how you can interpret that style outside. Where the mood is period, for instance, suggest the same feel in a design that accommodates period features, such as a stone bench or a fountain that is grand in feel.

## Strengthening the link

Now consider color. Is there a strong color scheme that would best be seen against a less demanding backdrop? Or is the room's effect neutral and able to take a strongly colored outside? Do you have a type of flooring inside, for example, that can be used outside? If not, consider what type of exterior paving will continue the feeling of the interior flooring. Then choose artifacts that will extend the mood. These guidelines should not become a straitjacket, however. Nobody is going to judge your garden for period authenticity. It is a place to indulge your whims and enjoy the results.

### 1 Glass and lighting

He looks happy enough above his little green oasis! To make the most of your small garden space day and night, year round, install as much glass looking into it as possible. Night lighting makes this a really viable additional room that is sheltered and can be used for many months of the year.

### 2 Planting

At the risk of using up too much valuable space, go for plenty of shrubby bulk, preferably evergreen. Don't worry about flower color— that comes later. Fragrance, though, is very important in limited space.

### 3 Furniture
A glass table with an interesting base and light, airy chairs do not become too dominant. These obviously work with the internal decor as well.

### 4 Bamboo
Ubiquitous bamboo makes a good evergreen plant that is not too heavy and can take some shade. Go for some of its decorative forms, such as *Fargesia murieliae*, which curves gracefully.

### 5 Ground cover
A simple ground cover preserves moisture, since if not irrigated, these tight urban areas get little rain and can be very dry. *Vinca* or periwinkle is a standard. I enjoy forms of *Lamium*, as well.

# Garden? What garden?

It is all very well, you might think, for those with neat little walled yards, but what about those with a drafty side entrance, a dark light-well, or only a window ledge—spaces that could never be called a garden, nor thought of as an outside room? Garden them in the traditional sense you cannot, but improve

them you certainly may. Because many such areas are initially unattractive, they are neglected and allowed to become dark, dank, or damp, particularly if they are below ground level. It may be that a flight of dingy basement steps is your only outside space. Rather than letting them detract from your surroundings, turn them into an asset—a pleasure to walk through and look at from inside or from the street. There are many different ways of enlivening unattractive places. Planting is one of them, but it shouldn't be the first option to spring to mind. Consider a lick of paint—use a vibrant color, paint a pattern, or even a *trompe l'oeil* (see page 67). Improve the flooring and the lighting, too. Left-over spaces that appear small on a plan are often contained by overpoweringly high walls. Consider a way of "bringing the ceiling down." Arbor beams may darken the space, but stretched ropes or wires are lighter, and you can run a foliaged climber over them, thereby creating a congenial space, albeit small, into which to escape outside for an evening drink.

"There are many **different ways** of **enlivening** unattractive places"

**Space to relax** (right) Careful use of color and natural materials has turned this small backyard into a restful area.

**No garden** (left)
Even the smallest space can be used—
the secret is not to garden it.

**Jungle problem** (below)
When gardened, the small space all too
quickly becomes a jungle.

**Vertical space** (right)
Growing plants on a wall allows more
space to move around at ground level
and adds visual interest at eye level.

## Doorstep and window gardens

The decorative potential of doors and windows that link us with
the outside world often remains unrealized. A few pots on a
window ledge and a colored window frame can act as a visual
extension to your room by breaking down the barriers between
in and out. If you live on a top floor, use your window to frame a
treetop view—if you don't have a garden, borrow one. The
technique for dealing with odd spaces successfully is not one of
cut-price gardening; rather, it is one of theater, where props,
illusion, light, and color can be used to create a lively place.

# Ideas for "no garden" spaces

Here are my proposed treatments for a townhouse with a basement (the office) and a small yard, a ground floor reception area and kitchen with a front door, a second floor main reception room with bedrooms above, and potential for a roof garden.

### 1 Front door
Carrying the decorative lines of the stucco wall on to the brick wall in wire to support plants, you create a wrap-around effect and reduce the dominance of the wall.

### 2 Planter
The brickwork is matched to resurface the entrance path with pavers, and to build a planting box with drainage, waterproofed so its contents will not dampen the wall.

### 3 Basement
The basement is paved to match the entrance to the front door above it, and the trees add interest from the street.

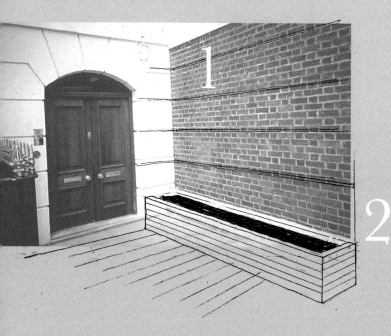

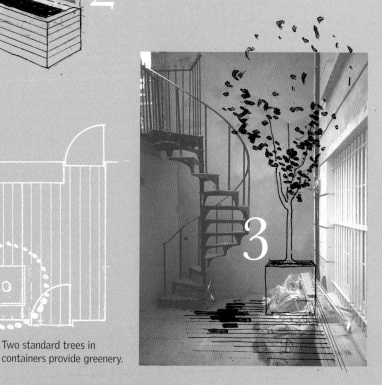

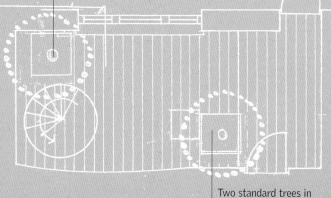

The basement is approached externally by a spiral staircase.

Two standard trees in containers provide greenery.

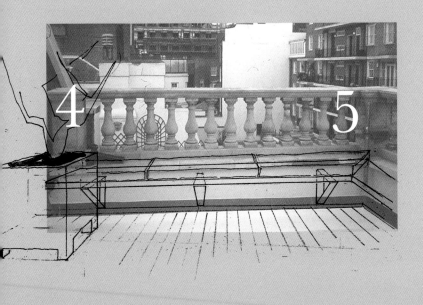

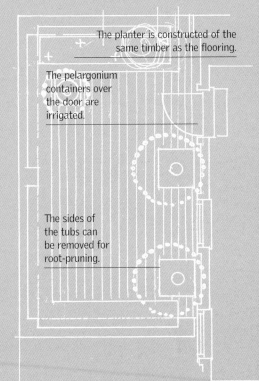

The planter is constructed of the same timber as the flooring.

The pelargonium containers over the door are irrigated.

The sides of the tubs can be removed for root-pruning.

### 4 Roof garden
The roof garden is floored with faded blue deck timber. There are two olive trees in fiberglass Versailles tubs.

### 5 Bench seat
A built-in bench seat is covered with rich blue canvas cushions, allowing for a table.

### 6 Roof-level planter
The planter contains evergreen *Pittosporum tobira* to create privacy and blue plumbago, which will flop around and flower all summer.

### 7 Over-door planter
Massed ivy-leaved pelargoniums are planted over the roof garden entrance door for a full and flowering effect. The garden is sheltered from killer winds.

**Before the transformation**
(top left) The existing fine flint wall running down one side of the garden.

(top right) The rear elevation of the brick-and-flint cottage, disfigured by drainpipes.

(bottom left) The existing garden access from the kitchen was cramped.

(bottom right) At the top of the garden and running across it was a utility building for a freezer and laundry room.

# A transformation

Located in southern England, the garden was stepped up behind the nineteenth-century brick-and-flint cottage, and at the top of the site was a huge timber chalet-type building—a deep freezer and laundry room. All essentials, but how to beautify? It seemed essential to take the eye away from the laundry, so I needed to create a central eye-catcher. Curving wing walls would emphasize this, but the current steps up to the usable part of the garden were far too meager-looking. By turning them around, they would become an additional feature and create a splendid landing for casual seating or on which to stand pots of this and that—the scrim of a garden.

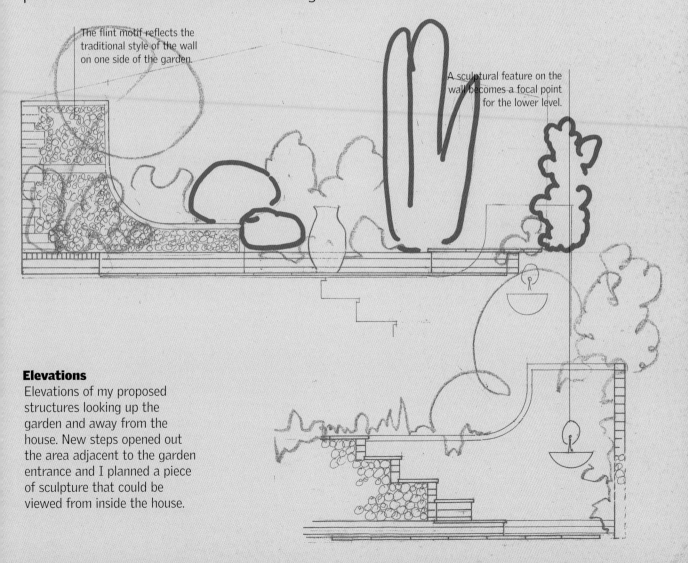

The flint motif reflects the traditional style of the wall on one side of the garden.

A sculptural feature on the wall becomes a focal point for the lower level.

**Elevations**
Elevations of my proposed structures looking up the garden and away from the house. New steps opened out the area adjacent to the garden entrance and I planned a piece of sculpture that could be viewed from inside the house.

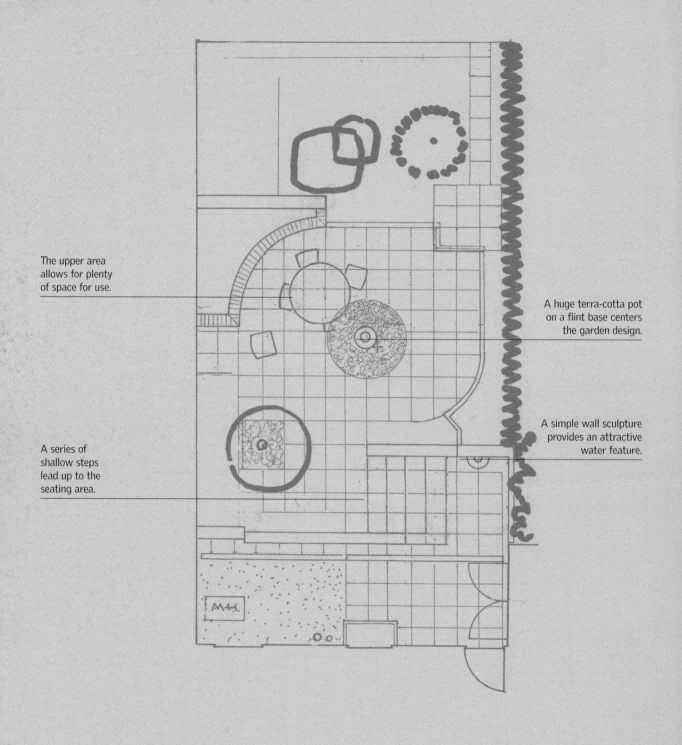

The upper area allows for plenty of space for use.

A huge terra-cotta pot on a flint base centers the garden design.

A series of shallow steps lead up to the seating area.

A simple wall sculpture provides an attractive water feature.

## Design

The whole layout had to be based around the size of the chosen paving slab, with as little cutting as possible. It is not the material that makes the structure of a garden expensive, but the labor involved. Since flint walls need a lot of man-hours, other labor had to be less time-consuming. The other important thing to remember is that a garden is a place for use, and since this was borne out in the brief from the owners, planting space was at a premium, too. This particular garden could be seen right through the house from the moment you opened the front door, and that had to be considered as well.

Adding to general construction expense was the need for all materials to be carried in through the house—there was no other access.

## Construction

You start by clearing the decks, getting rid of accumulated junk, such as old pots, worn-out bird feeders, and broken trellises. Then you peg out the design for the client to appreciate it, since drawings often mean little. You take levels, strip the sod, and start to dig, setting aside all existing topsoil, however poor, for reuse (it can be revitalized). The subsoil and rubble were moved out through the house.

Slowly, planes are created, footings dug, poured concrete foundations laid, and walls constructed. At long last, the paving goes down. The odd piece initially selected doesn't necessarily look well *en masse*, but it worked—picking up the blue of the flint. The steps from the house finish it all off very nicely.

**Details** (right, top to bottom) The top wing wall is completed with brickwork edging the flint—the lower wall will be plastered and painted; the terra-cotta pot sits on a circle of "knapped" or cut flints; the terrace and steps are of a bluish precast concrete slab, to work with the flint—note that the step tread overhangs the brick-and-flint riser.

## Planting

This is the stage everyone rushes to complete, inevitably too soon, and before the tailoring of the garden is complete. In this case, we had to work around the plants that existed, which weren't many, and to consider what to introduce to this calcareous soil. But before that, the soil levels in the beds were made up, reusing the stockpiled topsoil and adding some organic conditioner to improve its general water-holding capacity. These small gardens over chalk dry out quickly, and can get very hot when so well sheltered.

My plant selection in this case was made very much with an eye to immediate results, and of course subjects were placed fairly close together to create a quick effect. Lilies (*Lilium auratum, Lilium regale*, etc.) are among the plants of my dreams. Brought in when in flower, they create instant magisterial effect. Roses were planted to smother walls, and pinks to flop and perfume.

**Room for planting** (below left) I rounded the corners of the shallow retaining walls that contained the planting, and planned for the coping on the wall to be used as a temporary seat; (below right) the steps provide room for pots of herbs.

**A** 2 *Viburnum tinus*
**B** 2 *Hosta glauca*
**C** Existing euonymus
**D** Existing conifer
**E** 1 *Solanum glasnevin*
**F** 1 st. *Prunus subhirtella* 'Autumnalis'
**G** Lilies
**H** 1 cl. *Rosa* 'Guinea'
**I** 3 *Kniphofia caulescens*
**J** 3 *Artemisia* 'Powis Castle'
**K** 1 *Pittosporum garnettii*
**L** 1 cl. *Rosa* 'Madame Gregoire Staechelin'
**M** 1 *Hedera canariensis* 'Gloire de Marengo'
**N** 1 *Elaeagnus ebbingei*
**O** 2 *Olearia macrodonta*
**P** 1 *Rosmarinus repens*
**Q** Existing pear tree
**R** 3 *Heuchera* 'Palace Purple'
**S** 2 *Convolvulus cneorum*
**T** 1 *Pittosporum tobira nanum*
**U** 1 *Buddleia alternifolia*
**V** 4 *Hebe pagei*
**W** 1 *Plumbago capensis*

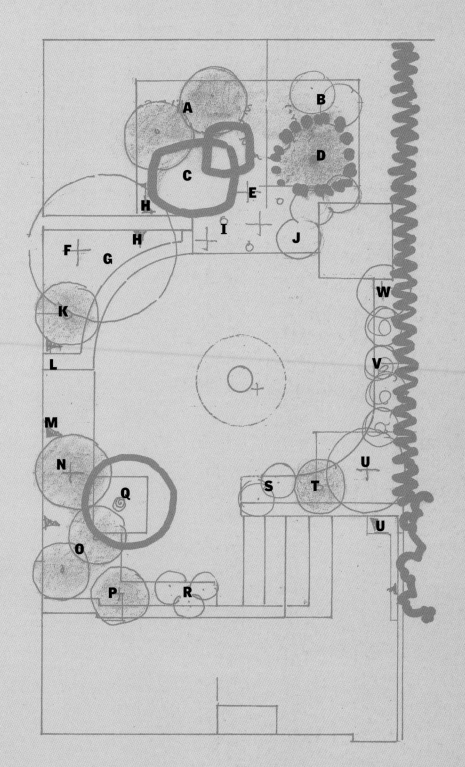

## Finished garden

The walls that were not flint were plastered and painted white. They lightened the place up. The small, curving wing wall seen from the front door, through the house, has a black-painted terra-cotta sculpture on it. I loved its simplicity and unpretentiousness.

We selected simple timber furniture, which will remain outdoors and will weather to a silver color. Bright lemon yellow cushions give the scene a lift.

The huge chalet structure across the top of the garden we stained dark, and given such alternative positive attractions—the seating, the large pots and the fountain—you really do not notice it anymore.

Scrim—that is, introduced pots and the like—I kept to a minimum, with only a small collection of herbs on the steps, suitably near the kitchen.

**Wall feature** (opposite) The very effective and simple wall fountain design. The self-circulating pump is located at the base of the fountain trough and water is pumped up through and up the back of the wall to come out of the mouth.

**Finished garden** (below) The complete effect, with a table beneath the shade of the existing old pear tree.

# style

The smallest of garden spaces should have style—a style that suits you and the way you live, as well as the character of your home and its surroundings.

**Cottage garden** (right) The classic English country cottage style has evolved, but is happiest in traditional settings.

# Room for style

"Style" is an evocative word that conjures up a galaxy of images, ranging from people and places to cars and clothes. I identify style in a garden space where there is a clarity of purpose that is derived from an aesthetically pleasing arrangement of shapes and patterns. Some styles might not be to your particular taste but, by virtue of the fact that they make a positive and coherent statement visually, you might happily acknowledge that they "have style." But how do you relate such abstracts to your small space when there are so many practical factors to take into account, such as the location and boundaries of the site, the style of your home, and most importantly, how you want to use the space?

The art lies in treating each element of your garden—be it the walls, furniture, steps, or a plant pot—as part of a single design. Always bear in mind how one relates to another in terms of color, shape, and texture, as well as function. A piece-meal approach—building a raised bed here, planting a shrub there—and an assortment of ill-considered bits and pieces will result in what I would consider an unstylish mishmash, and will also make a space seem smaller. A successful small garden, whether it be at ground level or on a balcony or rooftop, is one in which all its elements, from the smallest to the biggest, are in accord. Do not let the size of your garden make you timid in your design. Be bold and give it style!

**Decorative chic** (above) The clean style statement here comprises two outside rooms with topiary hedging and trained limes (*Tilia* spp.) to give enclosure. There is simple planting of *Agapanthus* in the foreground.

"Treat each **element** as part of a single **design**"

# What makes a style?

Understanding the essence of a look is the secret to breathing style into your small garden. As the photographs on these pages show, the cottage garden style (to take one very popular garden style as an example) can be interpreted in different ways. There are no sets of rules or clever formulas that govern how this is done. Instead, the art lies in having sensitivity to an overall picture and how detail fits into this.

**Contemporary cottage** (above) New cottage garden planting techniques owe something to the prairie or meadow combination of plants. Mixed forms, shapes, and colors create a mosaic, all planted in gravel, which acts as a mulch, preserving moisture.

# "a few characteristics effectively combined"

### Understanding a style's hallmarks

The classic cottage garden has a rural image of roses rambling around a door, and relaxed country planting. Many gardeners try to emulate this style, but all too often they miss their mark and find themselves with just a messy hodgepodge of planting. This is because the apparently relaxed disorder of country planting has to be controlled, for it is contained within a strong underlying framework. In the true cottage garden, the color of walls, paint, and roofing, and the texture of brick, clay, or stone, are all strongly evident. These strong structural elements are overlaid by soft, gentle, masses of plant material. The cottage garden look, whether it be in Devon, England, or Long Island, is created by the combination of the shapes, textures, and colors of hard materials with the soft ones of plants. Local building materials, artifacts, and native plants will give each a distinct character, but the hallmarks of the style are the same.

**Traditional urban** (top)  This more traditional urban cottage garden approach is planted with a continuous and mixed cycle of shrubby materials, perennials, and bulbs.

**Artful clutter** (bottom)  The simple act of gathering what you have grown in traditional baskets gives cottage gardening, on whatever scale, an added dimension and sense of achievement.

## Interpreting style

Feel free to extract the essence of a style and interpret it in your small garden. A well-known look can quite easily be given an amusing twist, such as using vegetables decoratively or including a light-hearted piece of sculpture. If your space is very limited, just a few of the characteristics of a style can be effectively combined. You might, for instance, group some brightly-colored cylindrical containers planted with yuccas for a high-tech feel, or use a mossy stone statue for a classical look.

### Soft evergreens

This garden has a modern Japanese feel, which would be increased when the doors to it are wide open. An evergreen bamboo clump (*Fargesia nitida*, also called *Arundinaria nitida*) sets the scene.

### Ground pattern

This garden has modern Amoeba-shaped islands planted with herbs to create a ground pattern through a granite paver terrace.

### 3 Focal point
A slate bridge crosses a shallow pool of water heavily planted with reeds and rushes.

### 4 Color and texture
The slate of the bridge is repeated in the horizontal of the table—a nice touch. *Agapanthus* and a *Hydrangea* in pots bring a bit of color to the scene.

### 5 Water feature
A word of warning for those with children: the shallowest water can be dangerous—though birds love it. A similar effect could be created with a dry pebble stream, with boulders. Elevate a water source for the birds.

# National garden styles

There are distinct national styles of garden—Italian, French, Spanish, Indian, Japanese, English, and central European, as well as those of the US, which can be loosely divided into East Coast, West Coast, Southern, desert, and prairie styles. Looking at how different styles have evolved is one way of introducing yourself to the many exciting ways of styling your outside space.

**Japanese** (left)
There is a calmness about the Japanese garden. It is to be looked at and contemplated. The object is to capture the essence of a natural association of plant and rocks.

**Mediterranean** (above)
The Mediterranean garden, on the other hand, is to be used. One lingers in its cool shade, and smells resinous cistus, rosemary, and pine. These gardens are hot and dry.

**Islamic** The Islamic garden is to be looked at and listened to. Pattern in the tile work is important, as is physical containment. The sound of moving water and simple plant forms soften the structural elements.

**Desert** The desert garden contrasts plants that will survive with the bare and often sandy spaces between them. Desert plants have adapted their forms to hold water and ward off hungry desert animals and birds.

## Reflecting building and life styles

The character of gardens around the world is closely linked to the local styles of building. The scale and shape of surrounding structures often give the garden character—low, flat buildings give an open look, tall narrow ones give an enclosed feel. Architectural idioms are often echoed in the detailing of a garden as well as the design of its layout. The color and texture of the materials used are an intrinsic part of the look, too. As well as echoing building styles, gardens reflect different ways of life and traditions. The design of the Japanese garden, for instance, has religious symbolism, while that of the North African garden, as well as providing a cool retreat from the heat, has a geometry and pattern that are traditionally Islamic.

**Brave new world** These Antipodean gardens demonstrate the use of local plants with strong forms to complement the contemporary straight-edged style of architecture and garden layout.

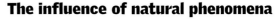

## The influence of natural phenomena

It is often native vegetation that gives us the strongest impression of place. Conifers and birch immediately make us think of cold climes, and palms and citrus trees of hot, dry locations. Vegetation is closely followed by the quality of light in a region. Strong light from a sun high in the sky creates hard-edged, deep shadows, whereas with a softer light we are more conscious of its warming glow. Closer to the poles, crisp sunlight from lower in the sky casts long shadows.

## "Ethnic" styles

I loosely term gardens that derive their style solely from the character of local features, such as the buildings, plants, and artifacts rather than a consciously-designed layout, "ethnic." The desert look is one of these styles. The African version, which takes its flavor from the beaten red earth, native pots, and tough plants, has counterparts in Rajasthan and Mexico. There is a tropical look, too, common to parts of Africa and the Caribbean.

"The **character** of gardens is closely linked to the local styles of **building**"

## Western styles

In the West, our images of different garden styles are linked to historical period as well as place. In the seventeenth century, European gardens had a formal layout, which was an extension of the logic of classical architecture. Formal Italian gardens thus have a distinct seventeenth-century feel. In the eighteenth century, an awareness of the Chinese garden and its abstracted, though natural, formation began to disconcert the European eye. When mixed with the increasing loosening-up of Baroque architecture, and the asymmetry of Rococo, the result was a more organic and flowing style of garden. The nineteenth century saw a mixture of formality and looser shapes, in gardens of a smaller scale. Among the myriad of contemporary styles there is the California outdoor-living look, first associated with the late 1950s, and the wildflower or prairie look, inspired by the loss of prairie habitat across America.

Although there is greater strength in a homogenous approach, the elements of distinct garden styles can be combined to a degree. A contrast of styles can work well, too. Such steps are sometimes successful when it comes to developing your own style, as you will see on the following pages.

**1 Lawn**
The lawn establishes the feel of an English-cottage-style garden at the entrance of a 19th-century American Victorian-style home.

**2 Tea rose**
Roses used to be a must in every garden. This form of hybrid tea rose has given way to easier-to-maintain shrub roses.

### 3 Climbing rose
The climbing and/or rambling rose is just as popular as ever.

### 4 Boxwood edging
The English gardener borrowed the idea of the boxwood edging of his beds from France, though boxwood has been constant since Roman times. Needing a small amount of clipping, boxwood adds neatness to a small area.

### 5 Gravel
A consolidated gravel path with timber edging is neat and tidy in a small space. Its use cuts down costs enormously— use a local gravel and roll a shallow layer into a prepared unwashed gravel base.

# What is your lifestyle?

It is not always easy, when faced with such a wide variety of garden styles, to decide which one would best suit your small yard. It is hard too, when looking at a site, to envision how it can be transformed into anything stylish. Looking at your personal style, and that of the building you live in, will point you in the right direction.

**Personal touches** (left) Garden furniture should reflect your own style and personality, and suit the purpose of your garden space.

**Central forms** (below left) This intricate piece of cast concrete paving focuses the eye to the center of its small space. A small fountain is almost incidental, while minimal seating is very undemanding.

### Interpreting your style outside

Seek to evolve a style outside that suits your personality, for your garden, like your clothes or your kitchen, should be an expression of your own taste. It may be that you go for the clear-cut look, or perhaps a relaxed, jumbled effect. An urban French couple, for example, might well find the randomness of an English garden hard to cope with, hating the apparent disorder, while, conversely, someone happy in this type of garden might find the clipped, classic order of a typical French garden too disciplined and restrictive.

The design of your garden should be suited to your lifestyle, too. Ask yourself how much time or inclination you have to tend plants. If you are green-fingered and enjoy nurturing plants, then provide yourself with plenty of greenery, room for your gardening equipment, and a table for potting. If, on the other hand, you have a hectic schedule that leaves little time for gardening, or you spend a lot of time away from your home, you would be better off with a garden that requires little maintenance. Such a garden relies on the textures and colors of its structure, and perhaps a *trompe l'oeil,* a piece of sculpture, and a few large plants in pots to provide the interest.

"The design... should be suited to your lifestyle"

**Seclusion** A corner in a small, lush green garden can work well as a retreat.

## Using your space

Decide also how you want to use your outside space. For instance, do you enjoy entertaining outside and want a table, chairs and a barbecue grill, or do you need space for your children to play, or even a small dog to run in? There are many ways of styling outside space so you can get maximum use from it. You might, for instance, have a space that gets little sun and is not very conducive to daytime use, but when planted with lilies and other scented plants makes a fragrant evening retreat. Or perhaps you have an urban roof space that gets full sun, but howling winds, too. Style a space like this to give you some shelter and also an air of privacy.

**Family life** A sandbox for small children (above left), though you need to cover the sandbox when not in use to keep cats out. A paved area (above right), however small, will provide a much-enjoyed play space.

## Looking at buildings

We live in a bewildering variety of structures, from urban townhouses to condominiums to apartment buildings, including every size of unit, and the infinite variety of suburban housing. The style of your home will probably have already influenced your choice of interior decorations and furnishings. Let it do the same for your garden. Every architectural style has idioms that can be expressed in the line and form of the garden's layout, whatever its size, and the selection of materials from which it is made, be it stone, cement, brick, or wood. The choice and grouping of pots and furnishings can be an extension of that style, as can the plants that soften the overall effect. You can be purist in your selection and historically accurate in each and every detail, or simply engender the general mood of a style.

# Gardens to live in

The notion that the garden, no matter how small or awkward the location, should be a place where plants reign supreme, or even a scaled-down version of a nineteenth-century country garden, is becoming increasingly impractical and outdated. The best use can be made of a small garden space if its structures—walls, steps, pools, and furniture—become attractive features of the garden in their own right, and plants, rather than dominating the garden or being its *raison d'être*, are used as decoration. By the time you have created a pleasant spot for eating in and another in which to sunbathe, the amount of space left for plants will have been considerably diminished. Introduce a fashionable hot tub, Jacuzzi, or plunge pool and the conventional image of the garden as a leafy retreat starts to take on quite a new form.

"Limit the number of objects and structures, and scale them up"

**Fireplace as focal point** (right)
"Feet up in front of a blazing fire"—nothing like it, on cool summer nights as the dew descends.

**Center-stage eating** (left)
A formalized terrace for a family meal where the table is definitely center stage.

## Increasing apparent size

As well as using space economically, there are many ways of increasing the apparent size of your small yard. A good first step is to extend the feel of the garden inside your home. For instance, placing tubs of plants on a small paved area, and on the floor of an adjoining room, will blur the division between inside and out. Using the same or similar tones of color on inside walls as you use on outside walls will have the same effect. It is an all-too-common misconception that small spaces are suited to an abundance of small objects. In fact, this usually creates a cluttered look and can make a very tiny enclosed space feel distinctly claustrophobic. As the art of the interior decorator shows, the fewer the number of objects in a small room and the simpler the range of colors and fabrics, the larger it will appear.

The same principle should be applied outside to create the same effect. Limit the number of objects and structures in your garden, and scale them up, rather than down. Stick to a simple range of materials, preferably matching them to existing structures, such as boundary fencing or the walls of your home. Build in as many features as possible and decorate the garden with a carefully chosen and limited selection of plants, grouped in bold masses.

**Total access** (above)
The more simple the concept, the more dramatic the effect. Deck lumber is again used in and out, but note the tiled effect on the right-hand side, running into the garden. The built-in seat finishes the "room outside" effect.

**Integrated space** (left)
A sliding door links a conservatory and its wood-decked garden. Similar light furniture and flooring with plants in as well as out, all help integrate the two spaces.

# Two-tier town garden

This small two-tier garden lies at the back of an English Edwardian townhouse. Originally, a rusty metal stairway led from a narrow balcony to a shabby grassed area below. Because there was no visual link between the two, they were viewed quite separately. The aim of the design was to unify the two, making the whole area appear more spacious and to create a stylish pocket of calm within a busy urban environment.

## Styling the new structures

The metal balcony and stairway were replaced by a new structure. Wood was used in order to forge a strong visual link with the timber door and window surrounds. The patterning of the crossbars is in the idiom of the architectural style of the house. Sage-green paintwork echoes the *Art Nouveau* flavor of the interior decor. The balcony was widened to accommodate chairs from the reception room from which it leads. The higher end section of the balcony railing, covered with a climber, screens the balcony from passers-by in the alleyway that runs alongside the house. At ground level, stone was chosen to replace the area of grass. Using hard surfacing unifies the area with the structure of the house; its mellow color blends in with the soft green paintwork. A climber growing up the balcony links the two tiers and, along with other plants and an existing tree, gives the garden an air of freshness. The overall effect is of a calm and simple retreat among urban surroundings.

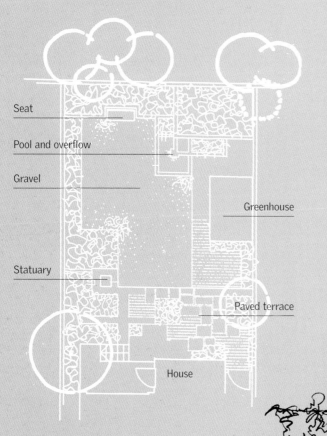

Seat

Pool and overflow

Gravel

Greenhouse

Statuary

Paved terrace

House

**Above** The garden plan.

**Right** The design concept sketched over the original rear elevation of the house.

### 1 Kitchen extension

The original angled bay window has become a kitchen extension with a door to the new balcony. The living room also opens to the balcony, with steps down to the garden terrace.

### 2 Balcony

The balcony was widened to accommodate chairs, with the higher end section planted to screen the space from passers by in the alleyway that runs alongside the house.

### 3 Terrace

The terrace was laid using random York stone paving.

### 4 Gravel area

The central consolidated gravel area is in fact under the spread of large overhanging trees that prohibited grass.

### 5 Pools and waterfall

A low- and higher-level pool are joined by a waterfall. A higher level still is planted with evergreens to screen the tennis courts beyond.

**Mirror trick** (left)
A tiny light well has been transformed
with a mirror on the rear wall. Two
simple containers containing yellow-
stemmed bamboo are doubled by
reflection.

**Simple plant show** (right)
Break up a hard-looking masonry corner
with hanging plants and pots of annuals.
There are plenty for both sun and shade.

# Gardens just to look at

The juxtaposition of buildings in towns and cities leaves many people with
small, awkwardly shaped and often unappealingly located spaces, which,
though visible from inside their homes, they cannot or have no inclination to
use as an outside room. Any such dingy yard, narrow passageway, or deep well
can be transformed from an area from which the eyes are hastily averted to
one that is a positive pleasure to look at.

## Decorating small spaces

There are many ways of bringing tiny spaces to life. Restricted light and difficult access often make gardening in the traditional way impractical, so instead of decorating your space just with plants, consider using colored paint, mirrors, sculpture, *trompe l'oeil* effects, and artificial light. It is important that the ground plan of your space should bear a relationship to surrounding structures, so start by looking at the paving. See if there are any architectural features on surrounding buildings that can be linked to the style of the paving— Victorian polychrome brickwork, for example, might suggest multicolored floor tiling.

Your next task should be to make the best use of the space by making it eye-catching. Using sculpture is one of the most simple and effective ways of anchoring the eye in a space (see page 232). Make sure that whatever you choose (be it a Classical stone statue or a modern abstract piece) has visual strength and is not dominated by its surroundings. Introduce the type of feature you might envision in a more open space, but go for as large a scale as you can to make the effect.

Plants are seldom visually strong enough to assume a sculptural role, nor in many cases are they a practical proposition where light is poor and their location makes regular maintenance a problem. However, given reasonable growing conditions, a gnarled fig tree might work, for instance, as long as the structure of its natural form is visually linked to the ground pattern and surrounding structures.

**Top** A striking Neo-Classical eye-catcher.

**Bottom** Water-slicked pebbles contrast with strong architectural leaf forms.

## Tricking the eye

*Trompe l'oeil* is an effective way of disguising reality and introducing a theatrical feel to a limited space. The Renaissance Italians were masters at providing amusing diversions, not only in their gardens, in the form of statues, but also visual tricks painted on their walls—a tiny monkey peering through a balustrade, or someone waving from an upper window. Similar techniques can be used to add an element of fun and magic to a space visible from your home.

Paint can be used in a simpler way, too. Colored walls can bring light and vitality to the most unappealing of spaces. Painting a space outside the same color as the room from which it is seen will make a strong link between the two. The reflections from strategically placed mirrors can trick the eye, too, making a space appear larger, or lighter, or to obscure an unwanted view. Artificial lighting is an effective way of enlivening a space that is dull during the day and giving it a magical touch at night (see page 237).

## Alternatives to planting

If growing conditions are too poor for real plants, or if the amount of space limits the number of plants you can grow, why not paint some o7n a wall? Alternatively, you can decorate your space with cut flowers arranged in a simply shaped container. Dried flowers can be striking, too, and can be left *in situ* for longer.

**Top** A whimsical wall container with a house name.

**Bottom** A painted pair of stepladders makes an amusing plant pot support.

# case studies

The four case studies featured on the following pages are of gardens that have been built over a period of 25 years or so. I hope that they demonstrate the usability and charm of small spaces well designed.

# My living space

The area now occupied by this garden was once used as a parking space, and the house it adjoins was a stable block. The new interior was designed first. A kitchen and living room, built in the downstairs area, were given sliding glass doors to allow easy access to the garden and to maximize the view of it from inside. The garden was designed to create an area that works as an open-air extension of the kitchen and living room, where outdoor meals are enjoyed and to which I feel closely connected when inside the house.

**View out** (left) The view from the kitchen outward is a constant pleasure. Ivy-colored arbor beams reach out underneath the canopy of a much-pollarded *Eucalyptus gunnii*. I put this in 25 years ago; the gray foliage matches the gray of the flint walls.

**Multipurpose terrace** (opposite) I am passionate about blue, particularly the shade I have chosen for the Adirondack-style chairs. Blue can go so well with gray, and green of course has blue in it. I potter around here, tending my plants.

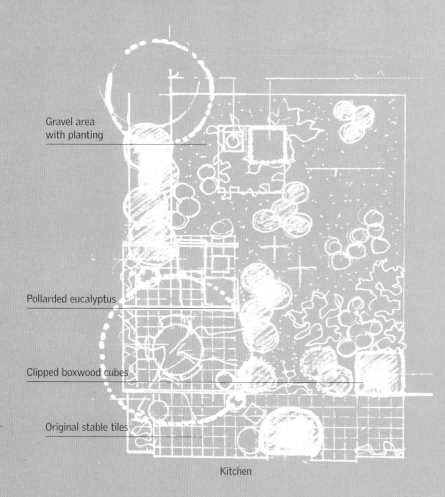

Gravel area
with planting

Pollarded eucalyptus

Clipped boxwood cubes

Original stable tiles

Kitchen

## 1 Reused materials

The building was originally a stable, and I have retained the stable tiles and gutter from the house on the left. These tiles were laid in a rhythmic pattern across an existing tiled drainage gully and into the area of new paving beyond the sliding doors of the house. Areas of pale brown gravel tone in well with the paving and contrast with planting in two brick-edged beds and in the gravel.

## Designing the structure

To make the area work as an extension, it was necessary to forge a strong link between inside and outside. This was done by echoing the dimensions of the kitchen in the terrace area. The kitchen ceiling is continued outside in the form of an arbor, the same height. The door, window surrounds, and arbor are all of the same unplaned, stained lumber. The arbor gives the area beneath it a pleasant roomlike quality, reinforced by the climbers that clothe the wall to its side. Two lights create a warm glow that gently illuminates the area, creating an atmosphere conducive to sitting outside on summer evenings, and enabling the area to be seen from inside the house at night, thereby maximizing enjoyment of the garden. The lights are especially appreciated during the winter months, when darkness falls early.

## 2 Outside painting

An outside painting on metal by Nigel Fuller. This is a new and interesting idea for a small-space decoration. Hanging adjacent to the terrace doors, the work can be viewed from inside the house, as well as presenting itself forcefully as you step outside.

## 3 Gravel area planting

In the gravel area adjoining the terrace I plant a variety of perennials and grasses, with bulbs for interest early in the year, to create a changing mosaic. In conjunction with the pale gravel and paving, the plants give the area a bright, sunlit feel.

## 4 Shrub border

Woody shrubs and trees continue this border. Seen here are *Phormium tenax* 'Variegatum', with *Pittosporum tobira* behind. To the left is the golden-leaved tree *Catalpa bignonioides* 'Aurea', which contrasts with the gray-foliaged pollarded eucalyptus.

# Gothic cottage garden

Having assessed the existing garden of a pretty Gothic cottage in London, I decided that it would be better suited to a semi-formal English-style design.

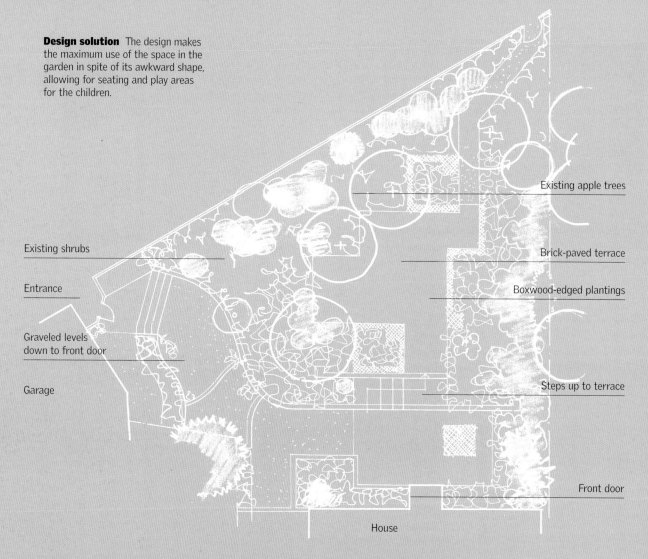

**Design solution** The design makes the maximum use of the space in the garden in spite of its awkward shape, allowing for seating and play areas for the children.

Existing apple trees

Existing shrubs

Brick-paved terrace

Entrance

Boxwood-edged plantings

Graveled levels down to front door

Garage

Steps up to terrace

Front door

House

## The plan

The garden is approached through a door in the wall near the garage. A small terrace gives a panoramic view of the garden before stepped gravel levels lead you down and across the garden to the front door. Brick steps up again opposite the front door lead to the brick-surfaced central terrace beneath existing old apple trees. The client is fond of topiary, so boxwood has been used to create an edging for central beds, with boxwood balls and pyramids punctuating the layout. In this way, the boxwood becomes part of the structure.

**Oil jar feature** (opposite top) The client already had a beautiful oil jar, which was relocated to become a feature in the far corner of the main brick terrace.

**Work in progress** (opposite) During construction, many of the existing plants had to be lifted and stored in temporary pots. Here, they are undergoing replanting.

## The works

The site had been mostly lawn, with a slope toward the house, making the lower area rather damp. This was solved by creating levels with brick retaining walls (making sure that tree roots were not disturbed), and by providing adequate drainage. To build steps running directly from the front door seemed too obvious, so I turned them to provide a standing ground for pots, and a casual seat on the edge of the terrace.

### 1 Main entrance

The path and stepped gravel terraces up to the main entrance to the house. An easy-to-get-at but discreet garbage-can enclosure is also situated near this doorway, off a small viewing terrace.

### 2 Lower terrace

The lower terrace is of consolidated gravel, to harmonize with stepped gravel terraces that connect it to the main entrance. Euphorbias and *Alchemilla mollis* grow well in this medium and are guaranteed to self-seed across it.

### 3 Brick steps

Brick steps lead up to the main terrace. They are wide and shallow enough to locate pots on them, and they link generous-sized landings at each 90-degree turn.

**4**

### 4 Main terrace

The main brick-paved terrace has been designed to be spacious enough for socializing, but also with an intimate corner for quiet contemplation. Existing mature plants and the boundary wall provide a secluded setting despite the urban location. Many of the plants that surround the terrace would not be considered half-hardy if the position was not so sheltered.

# An apartment garden

This small garden is L-shaped, and it surrounds the ground-floor apartment of a single, retired woman. She is not particularly interested in gardens or gardening, so permanent evergreen planting and hard surfacing seemed to be a good solution to the maintenance problem, while also providing a measure of privacy and a place for occasional quiet relaxation.

However small, an L-shaped plan will always give multiple views and maximum design options. Here, the garden splits into the apartment entrance area and a more secluded side—the obvious location for a seating area. Both areas can be seen from the entrance gate, but each is designed to retain its own discreet charm.

**Seating area** (opposite) The seat has been placed to catch as much of the sun as possible, with a small tree and hedge providing some screening from the neighbors.

### 1 Paving
Precast concrete slabs form a path across the garden in this view, and also provide a sitting place to the side of the apartment. The remaining surface is laid with compacted gravel and is planted randomly with various species that enjoy free drainage.

### 2 Mature planting
A good proportion of the plant material is evergreen for year-round enclosure, and after 10 years there is a sense of maturity. Pots are grouped for herbs and "a bit of color."

### 3 Structural plants
I selected structural plants with strong architectural forms to make a contrast with the rigid lines of the building. The tree on the wall is the loquat, *Eriobotrya japonica*, which barely fruits in this northern temperate location.

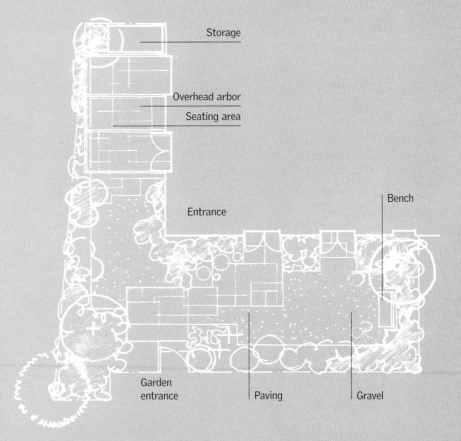

Storage

Overhead arbor

Seating area

Entrance

Bench

Garden
entrance

Paving

Gravel

## Designing the garden

The plan of the garden "gridded up" very neatly. Most buildings
are conceived around a module—a key measurement that
regulates distances between doors, windows, and other
structural divisions. You can often establish what this module is
by running a measuring tape along the external walls, noting the
distances between doorways and window openings. Using your
estimate of what the module is to give yourself a guiding grid for
your design is particularly useful in such a small space. It will
allow you to be bold about establishing the scale of each element
of the plan.

Notice my use of paving in the plan. It provides a direct route
from garden gate to apartment entrance, but its ground pattern
encourages you to meander if you want to linger in the garden
and enjoy it. The gravel surfacing beyond allows for further
appreciation of the plants and access to an inviting bench.

# Country style in town

This small, country-style garden lies cheek to cheek with the cathedral at the ancient heart of a southern English city. The owner, who had moved from a country home with a large garden, wanted a similar style of garden in which she could tend and nurture plants—her passion—albeit on a much-reduced scale.

**Traditional style** (left) The often piecemeal development of houses in older cities is part of their charm and calls for a garden styled to match.

**Exceptional view** (right) The garden is located next door to a cathedral, so the views out are extraordinary and demand a sympathetic treatment.

## The site

When I first visited this garden, some years ago, the house had recently been extended. A step (approximately 20 in/50 cm) led up from a terrace of random paving to an area of rough grass—very rough, in fact, since it was used as a dumping ground during alterations to the house. Beds bordered the surrounding walls. An open area was needed, on which to stand furniture, so the paved area adjacent to the house was retained. Visually, too, it was important to keep one area free as a contrast to the spectacular array of plants with which the owner planned to fill the rest of the garden. With this in mind, the aim of the design was to create a structure that would contain and steady the mass of soft, country-style planting without dominating it, and that would blend in well with the surroundings. The looser and more relaxed the style of planting, the more important it is to have a structure of hard materials and strong skeleton plants that will prevent it from becoming a jumble. By contrast, in small gardens where the owner's priority is to use the space for activities other than gardening, plants are introduced primarily to soften the strong lines of hard materials of the structural elements.

**Garden door** (top right) This door is the main entrance into the garden, so a visitor's first view is all suffused with the scent of climbing roses in summer, and the soft gray and blue of lamb's-ears and lavender.

**Burgeoning plants** (right) The design depends on plants spilling out of beds and pots to create a really relaxed atmosphere.

## The ground pattern

Only one of the existing border beds, and part of another, were retained. All the grass was taken up and replaced with a combination of gravel, stone, and brick. Brick was used to build a gentle step up from the paved terrace adjacent to the house, edge the beds, and make a few simple divisions within the rest of the site. A coating of pale, washed gravel was rolled into a 2-in (5-cm) layer of unwashed binding gravel; this makes a textural contrast with the plants grown in it. Old paving slabs and brick, the color of which complements that of the gravel and of the house, were laid at various points throughout the graveled area to make a path through the garden and give easy access to the plants. Their geometrical patterns contrast with the loosely structured style of the planting.

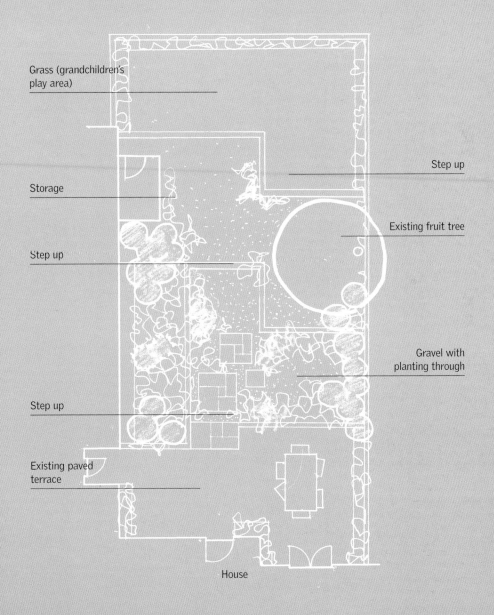

Grass (grandchildren's play area)

Storage

Step up

Step up

Existing paved terrace

House

Step up

Existing fruit tree

Gravel with planting through

## Country-style planting

The abundance of plants and their loose arrangement form a gentle, billowing outline, typical of the country garden. Caring for a variety of plants is time-consuming, so this style of planting is suited only to those who, like the owner of this garden, are happy to devote time to them. The harmonious, calm quality of the garden comes from the arrangement of groups of a particular plant in coherent "drifts." Dotting plants around the garden, one here and one there, would have created a restless, un-unified appearance. Great care was taken in the combination of colors. The greens, grays, and golds of foliage act as a restful backdrop to the stronger, seasonal colors of the flowers.

## Structural shrubs

Evergreen shrubs such as *Mahonia japonica* and the near-evergreen *Viburnum x burkwoodii* give structure to the planting and provide interest during the months of winter. Their dark green foliage contrasts with that of gray plants such as *Senecio* 'Sunshine', *Hebe pinguifolia* 'Pagei', and *Lavandula angustifolia*, and the purple-bronze leaves of *Ajuga reptans* 'Burgundy Glow' and the red winter stems of *Cornus alba*.

## Leafy shrubs

Deciduous shrubs including *Philadelphus coronarius* (mock orange), which has pointed oval leaves, and a variegated *Cornus alba* swell the shape of the garden when they are in leaf.

## Country-garden scent

One of the great attractions of the country garden is its scent. Here, roses give a sweet summer aroma, along with the delicious orange-scented blossoms of *Philadelphus coronarius*. These are supplemented by the herb-garden scents of catmint, lavender, balm, and marjoram. The lily-of-the-valley-fragranced blossoms of *Mahonia japonica* scent the garden from fall to midspring. The country fragrance of the garden can be enjoyed from inside, too, since a climbing rose surrounds the doors and windows, and catmint grows beside the house. Butterflies and bees, attracted by the profusion of fragrant and colorful plants, add to the pleasantly countrified atmosphere of the garden.

## Linking colors

Traditional country garden plants, including roses, are grown together in carefully orchestrated drifts of color. In the left-hand bed, for example, catmint (*Nepeta x faassenii*), stock (*Matthiola incana*), and *Aquilegia* spp. make a billowing summer combination of gentle mauve, pink, and white. The bold evergreen foliage of *Bergenia cordifolia*, which grows among these, gives strength to the planting and provides interest when the flowers die away. This gentle color scheme is continued throughout the rest of the garden by the pink rose (*Rosa* 'Comte de Chambord'), white rose (*Rosa* 'Pearl Drift'), and pink valerian (*Centranthus* spp.).

# design

Putting pen to paper and planning the layout of your small space in detail will enable you to get the most from it, both visually and physically.

**45-degree effect** (opposite) The drama of this decked garden is all in its 45-degree design.

# Creative planning

You may find the thought of designing anything, let alone a garden, daunting, seeing it as the sole preserve of those "in the know"—some amorphous body of aesthetes. Yet each time you decide how to arrange some ornaments on a shelf or where to position a sofa, you are influenced by the basic principles of design: practical considerations such as ease of cleaning or the location of a light, as well as aesthetic ones, such as the appearance of an object's shape, texture, and color in relation to surrounding objects and surfaces. In the same way as

you arrange objects in a room to make a pleasing yet functional composition, you can arrange the elements of a small garden, counterpoising an area of paving, for instance, with one of water, gravel, and planting. Good design will give you maximum pleasure from your small space, since the closer the bond between the different elements in it and its surroundings, the larger it will appear. The basic techniques of design are explained on the following pages, and then the use of color, shape, and special effects are explored. With all this under your belt and some ideas from the Special Design Cases, you can go on to tackle the design of your own space, however small, and whatever its location.

**Perfect balance**
The balance of interest between seating and planting is excellent in this garden. The two elements are connected by a fascinating timber screen/wall detail.

**Architecture rules** A really crisp minimal solution to outside living in a very small space, with 75 percent architectural to only 25 percent horticultural.

PLANNING YOUR SPACE

# The design process

The design process consists of several stages: assessment (of the site and your requirements), measuring up, drawing to scale, evolving a pattern, and translating your pattern into areas of structure and planting. The design of a small town garden is taken as an example and illustrated on this and the following pages in this section.

### Assessing the site

First, look carefully at your site, ask yourself plenty of questions, and note any problems. For instance, is it overshadowed by neighboring buildings or a tall tree? Which areas, if any, get the sun? Are there any eyesores you would like to disguise? Then ask yourself how you want to use the space. Do you enjoy gardening and want to devote most of the space to plants? Or do you want an area that requires minimal maintenance? Would you like to be able to use the space for parties, or do you need a play area for children?

**Vision of the future** (below) Take a flight of fancy and try to visualize what you would like to see in your garden in a year or two.

"**look** carefully at your site; ask yourself plenty of **questions**"

## The design brief

The brief for this garden was that it was to be very usable and visually attractive at all times of the year, since it and the house on two sides of it were inseparable. Being sheltered by a 10-ft- (3-m-) high wall, the garden gets very hot, though the owners were not sun-lovers and what was wanted was a cool, green jungle. Well, jungles in England don't happen overnight, but this space has now been planted up for a year—and we're getting there!

## Measuring up

First, draw an outline sketch of the site on which to note your measurements. Then measure across the width of the house wall facing the garden, including any adjacent structures, and then measure the length of your site at an angle of 90 degrees from each side of this. If the far end of the site is narrower than the house, measure back to the house from each end of the boundary facing it. Make a note of the dimensions of permanent features (such as trees or a pool) and their distance from the house and boundaries, and the height of the doors and windows and their distance from one another and the boundaries. As well as brandishing your measuring tape, and it was no big deal here, make notes to yourself, preferably throughout the day and evening, to establish just what is sunny and shady—in short, the direction of north and south.

**Nearly blank canvas** (top right) This particular courtyard was as the builder had left it. Surrounded by a 10-ft- (3-m-) high wall, the site was flat and grassed.

**Drawing a plan** (right) Note your measurements, labels, and other details on a simple outline sketch, then draw up a plan to scale, as carefully as you can.

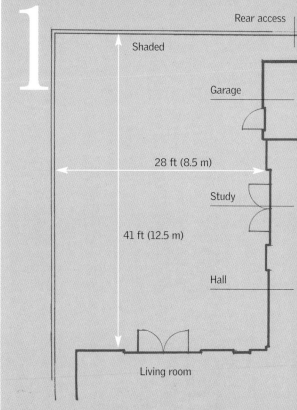

1

Rear access

Shaded

Garage

28 ft (8.5 m)

Study

41 ft (12.5 m)

Hall

Living room

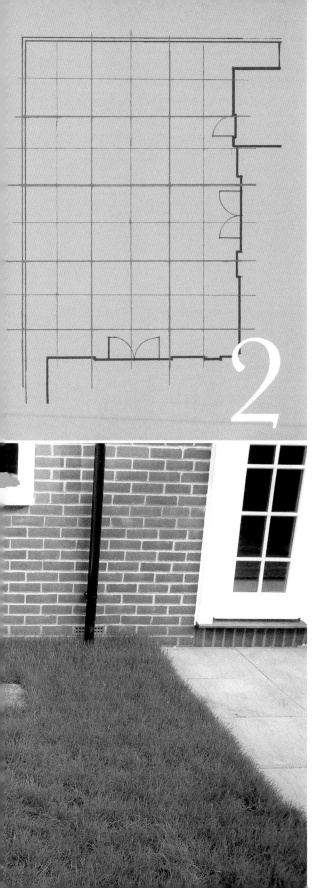

## Drawing up

The next stage is to draw up an accurate scaled plan of your garden. Use a scale of 1:50 (one unit of measurement on your plan for every 50 in your garden), or 1:25, whichever fits on your size of paper. Using the measurements you have taken, draw in the boundaries and the exact position of any existing features (such as steps or areas of planting) you intend to keep. Scaled rules are widely available and will speed up this process.

## Making a grid

You can now devise a grid that will make any pattern you choose to fit into it suit the proportions of your home and its garden space. On tracing paper (so that you can overlay your scaled plan and compare different patterns), draw up a series of squares that relate in size to the dimension of a permanent feature of the house or in the garden—the width of a door or height of a window, or the width of a step, for instance. In this garden, the main feature of the house is its two sets of double doors, approximately 10 ft (3 m ()) wide. If you extend lines from each set of French windows, you will achieve a square in the middle of the plot; this then becomes your grid scale and its lines can be repeated. You will get leftover bits along the bottom of your grid, but this doesn't matter. If you now halve your basic grid in both directions, you have made your own graph paper, as it were, suited to your particular site.

**Devise a grid** (top left) Draw your grid on a separate sheet of tracing paper and use it beneath the tracing paper sheets you use to evolve your design.

**What lies beneath** (left) Square paving and turf await the construction phase. What lurked under the turf and slabs was a mystery. So all lay ahead.

## Evolving a pattern

The next stage is to evolve a pattern using your grid, and pieces of paper that relate in size to the grid squares. For example, some pieces of paper can be half the size, some the same size, and some double the size of the grid squares. Use the squares to create a pattern on your grid, rather like a collage. Whatever the pattern you create, it will have a proportional relationship back to the house or boundary; in this example, the pattern will have a

relationship to the bay window and thus the living room, which opens out on to the garden.

Try the squares at right angles to the house or at 45 degrees to it, or a combination of the two. If you want a garden pattern on the oblique (and this is a good way of breaking up the boxiness of a small garden), turn all the cut shapes at an angle of 45 degrees. In a small space, any angle smaller than 45 degrees or larger than 90 degrees is likely to create awkwardly shaped areas that will prove

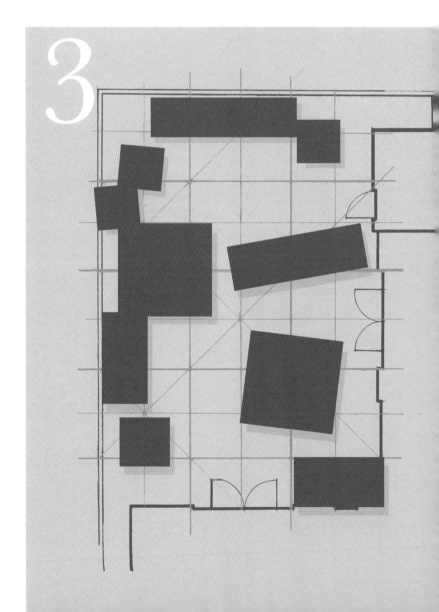

**Use collage to experiment** (right)
The next stage is to evolve a pattern using your grid and pieces of paper that relate in size to the grid squares. For example, some pieces of paper can be half the size, some the same size, and some double the size of the grid squares. Use the squares to create a pattern on your grid.

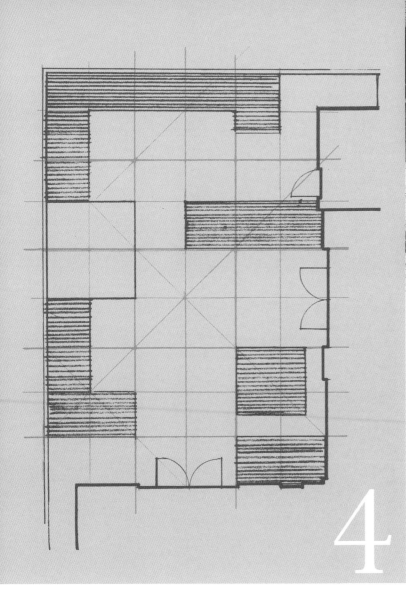

**Ground work** (above) Work in progress as all the existing sod is stripped off.

**Relating shapes** (left) While you are arranging your shapes, bear in mind your requirements and try to imagine what form the shapes might take in reality, how they would relate to each other, and how they might look from inside at ground level and from any rooms above.

4

difficult to deal with as an element of the garden, be it pavement, planting area, water, or whatever.

Some people consider straight lines to be unsympathetic, and would prefer to use curves, but bear in mind that if the proportions are correct and the area is well planted, the straight lines will be softened by vegetation. If you want curved structures, substitute circles cut out so that their diameters equal the length of one of the sides of your grid squares, or a fraction or multiple of it.

When designing a garden enclosed by walls (as many small-space gardens are), it is all too easy to be tempted to use the boundary walls as a starting point, running a raised bed all the way around them, for instance, only to emphasize the garden's shortcomings. By using the collage method, you will avoid this temptation, since your shapes will relate to the house and one another.

## Realizing your design

Once you have a design that you find visually pleasing and that seems broadly to fulfill your practical requirements, start to knock it into shape by defining exactly what form each area will take in reality. In the example illustrated on these pages, the possibility of using the space between the pattern and the boundary for planting has already been considered; but what about the rest? What is to be the main feature of the garden, what should be used to screen the oil tank, which areas should be paved, and what materials should be used for the paving and the new retaining walls?

**Developing the concept** (below) You begin to get the feel of the garden as the design concept progresses.

**The structure on plan** (right) Having defined what is hard-paved and what is soft planting, one needs to hammer out the detail. An arbor will provide some shade and become a feature until the planting takes over. Raised beds against the wall will help to reduce their height. A raised bed for planting outside the hall window, opposite the front door, will make another feature. The rest of the pattern is a collage of brick steps filled in with stone paving.

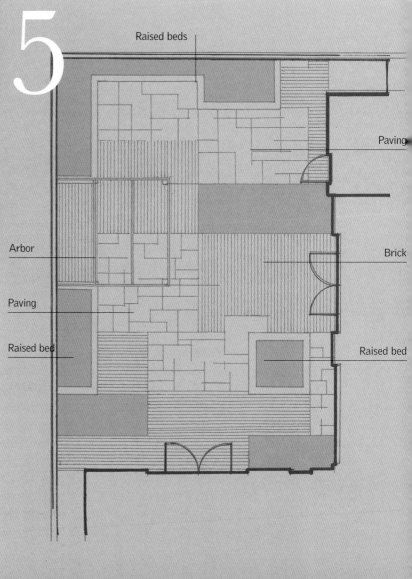

Raised beds

Paving

Arbor

Brick

Paving

Raised bed

Raised bed

### 1 Raised beds
Raised beds in brickwork to match the surrounding wall and wall of the house, built to seating height for parties. Each bed, and the wall behind it, is waterproofed, with adequate drainage outlets below.

### 2 Arbor
The arbor is constructed of stained softwood sitting on metal verticals, those on the outer edge with a slightly decorative capital. Wires will extend between the boards as the climbers it hosts become more rampant.

### 3 Paving
The paving is a mixture of Indian stone, which is a relatively inexpensive stone, and hard paving brick. All is laid on a concrete base, with a drainage channel from the house running into areas of planting.

## Plants and the design

When a layout such as this is newly completed, it will look extremely hard, but this effect will be beautifully softened by the introduction of plants. The styling of the plant material and its overall shape, color, and texture should relate to the style, shape, color, and texture of the garden's structure and the interior of any rooms that adjoin the garden.

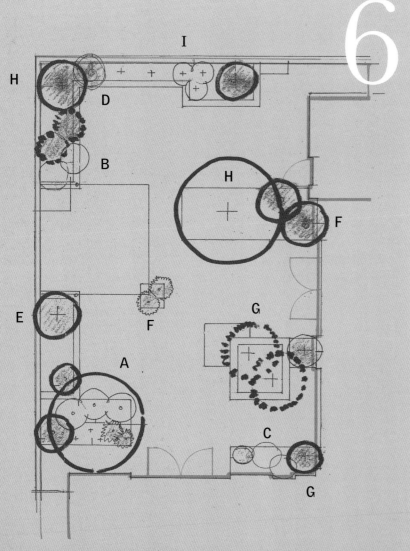

A *Iris pseudacorus*
B *Lonicera nitida* 'Baggesen's Gold'
C *Symphoricarpos orbiculatus* 'Foliis Variegatis'
D *Hypericum x inodorum* 'Ysella'
E *Chrysanthemum parthenium*
F *Digitalis grandiflora*
G *Melissa officinalis* 'Aurea'
H *Primula bulleyana*
I *Lysimachia nummularia*

**Planting plan** (left) Finally, you need to draw up a basic planting plan. Since this garden is situated in southern England and is so sheltered, a proportion of the plants used here are not very hardy and would not necessarily flourish in colder regions.

### 1 One year later
The garden one year after it was planted is already beginning to look full. I had intended to feature a standard tree and possibly some sculpture in the garden. The poodle-cut boxwood fulfills both these functions admirably.

### 2 Bed maintenance
Beds are overflowing, which softens the edges and creates that desirable relaxed effect. Such a garden will need quite firm maintenance in the way of cutting back as it continues to mature over time.

### 3 Effect from inside
Fan palms create interest on entering the house when seen through the entrance hall. The impact of this particular type of garden space is just as important from inside the house as from within it.

# Color

Color, like sound and smell, has the power to strengthen mood. While there is no need to be specific about color as you evolve the design for your space, you should be thinking about its overall "feel" and how this can be expressed in color. The location of your site, the materials from which it is built, its exposure (whether it is sunny or not), its usage, and the style of any adjoining rooms will suggest the mood.

"Color, like sound and smell, has the power to strengthen mood."

## The effects of color

Some colors are soothing and calming, others stimulating and invigorating—choose the ones that you empathize with and that reinforce the mood of your garden space. A small, sunny terrace with a Jacuzzi, for instance, is a high-activity space that would be best suited to invigorating blues and yellows rather than purples and grays, which would be too lugubrious. On the other hand, too much orange and puce would be out of place in a small country-style garden, with a gentle, quiet air that would be enhanced by colors with a calming quality, such as white, cream, and soft blues, pinks, and greens.

## Creating a color scheme

It is particularly important that colors work well together in a small space, since every garden element, from walls and paving to furniture and planting, will be close together and viewed as a whole, and will quite possibly be seen in conjunction with the colors inside your home. Create a color scheme for your outside space as you would a room inside, coordinating each part of it.

Select your plants by looking closely at a plant catalog, or better still, visit a garden center or plant nursery with pieces of

## Judging the effects of light

Light affects the quality of color, so bear in mind what the colors you choose will look like at different times of the day. Pale colors look pleasingly soft in gentle morning and evening light, but can appear washed out in a strong, noonday sun. Conversely, colors strong enough to cope with a high-noon sun can look too garish in the morning and evening. Put pieces of colored paper in sunny and shady spots and note the effects that the light has on them at different times of day. Try, too, to visualize what the colors you choose will look like in relation to seasonal changes of color—for instance, the fresh, clear shades of spring and the strong, rich shades of fall.

**Orange splash** (top, left) A bright splash of orange helps to contain this terrace visually, and would certainly brighten it up in winter.

**Seasonal color** (top, center) Choose your plants carefully so that they provide the desired colors at the right time of year.

**Textured color** (below left) Colored stains can be used on fencing or on flooring, allowing the grain of the wood to show through.

**Watery shades** (below) Gentle coloring featured on the wall beyond this pool gives added interest to the foliage shadows.

# Shape and pattern

It is the shapes used in your design and the pattern they make that will set the tone of your garden's style. There are endless permutations with, at one end of the spectrum, the symmetrical arrangement of shapes that will give your space a formal, classical look, and at the other, an asymmetrical arrangement of shapes that has an abstract, modern style—each suits different situations.

**Curved** (above left) Use generous curves; if they will not fit into your small area, they are probably not the solution.

**Right-angled** (above) House walls and garden boundaries usually suggest 90-degree patterns, here realized in a rill.

"You can **arrange** your shapes to create a sense of **movement** or **repose**."

**Abstract but linear** (opposite) An interesting formal layout with an abstract (though still linear) design in boxwood, gravel, and timber working across it.

## Shapes for small spaces

Given that many urban spaces are surrounded by structures at 90 degrees to one another, rather than flowing boundaries of fields and trees, a design of geometrical shapes with straight lines is usually most appropriate. However, circles, segments of circles, or curved lines can work, as long as they are arranged within a right-angle grid (see page 98 on using a grid for design).

In a small area, the most effective designs are usually produced by using one type of shape—rather than mixing diagonals and curves, for example—since the limitations

of space will not usually allow you to extend such a design to its logical conclusion.

You can arrange your shapes to create a sense of movement or a sense of repose. Linear shapes and patterns give a sense of movement by leading the eye. In a small space, it is important that free, curved shapes have a purpose (unless the boundaries are curved) by leading the eye to a feature such as a piece of statuary within your space, or even to something outside it, such as a tree in the yard next door. Static shapes can be arranged in patterns that will hold the eye within the site; these are usually more restful and are suited to enclosed spaces where there is no focal point.

**Unifying squares** (top) A regular pattern has been carried all the way through this garden terrace, with even the loungers fitting the scheme.

**Soothing curves** (left) Gently curved structures create a relaxed mood when built in natural stone.

### 1 Surface interest

When curves are used in too small a space, the result can look forced and artificial. But since it is arguable that a garden in such a limited area is just that, why not go with the flow? Differing types of surfacing here create visual interest: deck lumber, paving, and water are juxtapositioned at various levels to create "rooms."

### 2 Impactful planting

Strong foliage forms work well when viewed from above. Where the space is exposed to wind, smaller-leaved species will avoid its shredding effect.

### 3 Space-saving seating

Built-in seating helps to save space where it is at a premium. Note the curving timber seat-back, which then forms the retaining boundary of a planter in the foreground. from above.

### Three-dimensional shapes

Two-dimensional patterns come alive when they are taken into the third dimension by deciding on the relative height of one shape to another and selecting the materials that will "fill" them. Giving some of the shapes height will immediately give definition to others, but think also of giving some of them depth—in the form of a sunken pool or seating area, for example.

### Materials

The qualities of the materials you select to "fill" these shapes will mold the character of your garden, too. You can choose from hard and soft materials, rough and smooth, light and dark, light-absorbent, and light-reflective, in the form of brick, concrete, grass, gravel, wood, and water.

**Raised planting** (left) With the added dimension of height, you start to create spaces or volumes, and proportion, mass, and void are brought into play.

**Geometry in boxwood** (above) A geometric pattern, with curving shapes enhanced by a curving background hedge and balls of boxwood.

# Special effects

There are a number of design tricks and devices, employing paint, trellis, mirrors, and the use of natural phenomena such as light and shadow, that can be used to decorate your garden and give it an exciting theatrical or dramatic flavour. Such techniques suit the character of man-made surroundings and can provide inventive ways of decorating spaces where conditions are too inhospitable for plants to grow; some can be used to create an illusion of size too.

**Mirrored obelisk** (below) A clever use of mirrors, which doubles the effect of, in this case, masses of flowers. Mirrors need regular cleaning, however; winged visitors can quickly destroy the illusion.

## Painted trompe l'oeil

The Renaissance Italians were the early masters of painted *trompe l'oeil*, creating lavish and apparently three-dimensional architectural scenes and rural idylls on walls both inside and out. Lively and colorful murals are often used to enliven the city landscape today – their subjects ranging from animated market scenes to window-boxes, palm trees, and bright abstract patterns.

Painted *trompe l'oeil* and decorative murals can be just as effective on a smaller scale. Why not paint a door to suggest another garden beyond your own, a window with a window-box (the window-box could be real) or plants and trees where the real thing cannot grow or to "thicken" up existing vegetation? Those who use their city garden only in the evening could create a dramatic night-time scene by painting the walls midnight blue with white flowers and gray foliage (real or painted); in combination with subtle lighting the combination would be spectacular.

Exterior grade paint should be used on garden walls. Different effects can be achieved by using matt or eggshell finishes and by perhaps using bold stencils and spray paint to create patterns as a focal point. When using paint you can afford to be brave in your design, for any real mistake can be painted over and a fresh start can be made.

**Tuscan memory** (opposite) a painted Tuscan hillisde fills a suitably Classical doorway. More a remembrance than a trick, any scene would work.

## Using shadow

Where the natural light is strong, position plants or architectural features where they will cast dramatic shadows on surrounding surfaces. An arbor's horizontals, for instance, can be constructed where the light will shine through them to produce a strong, geometric pattern of shadows, or plants with architectural form, such as *Euphorbia characias wulfenii*, placed in front of a plain background, such as a wall, which will display their shadows to great effect.

If the light is not strong enough to produce strong shadows, why not paint some on surrounding surfaces? Use different tones of the same color to imitate shadows of varying intensity, remembering that the brighter the sun, the deeper the shadows will be.

**Fence and foliage drama** (opposite top) Bamboo leaf shadow dances across the horizontal strips of ranch fencing.

**Grille effect** (opposite bottom) Australian designer Jack Merlo used an intricate grille to cast a dramatic shadow in this show garden.

**Bamboo shade** (above) Bamboo makes an ideal lightweight sun screen and casts a shadow that appears to texture surfaces beneath.

**Behind the door** (above right) Shadow is an integral part of this composition, suggesting an inner place of rest.

"position features
where they will cast
dramatic shadows"

## Using mirrors

Reflections in glass and water can be used to create an illusion of size. Strategically placed mirrors, by reflecting the area you already have, can double the size of your garden visually, or even, if correctly positioned, create the impression of an ever-receding space. Large areas of mirror are an effective way of brightening areas such as shaded basements or dark wells between city dwellings.

Always use mirrors at least ¼ in (6 mm) thick and prepare them for use outdoors by lining the back with silver foil to protect the coating and mounting them on wood; the edges should be sealed to keep out moisture. Only place mirrors in a shaded position so there is no risk of reflected sunlight singeing your plants, and remember that they must be sparkling clean to be effective.

Mirrors can also be used to draw attention to a special feature such as a statue or a collection of topiary. They produce an especially atmospheric effect in deeply shaded corners, where they reflect the little light there is.

## Reflections in water

A small pool of water, however shallow, will make your space appear larger. You can use a light-absorbent liner, such as black plastic, which will make the water surface reflect the surroundings like a mirror, while creating the impression of infinite depth. Alternatively, you can use light-reflective materials, such as mirror tiles, to reflect overhanging features, such as a piece of sculpture or some eye-catching plants, and increase the amount of light in your garden. A mirror alongside, to reflect the reflections in the water, will increase the visual excitement further and give your space an impression of size.

**Mirror in trellis** (above) Even a modest-sized mirror, here set in a trellis screen, will transform a tiny space, illuminating it as well as increasing its apparent size.

**Reflective materials** (opposite, top) The backrest and underseat areas of this recessed seating area are reflective, creating an illusion of greater expanse.

**Mirror pool** (opposite, bottom) Using a black liner turns a pool of brimming water into a mirrored surface, reflecting available light into a small space.

SPECIAL DESIGN CASES

# Basements

Below-ground-level living is becoming more and more common as large, old houses are divided into smaller units. The outside area left to basement homes often consists of a small space wedged between street level and front door, or a small, sunken backyard. Towered over by the walls of adjacent buildings, they tend to be gloomy and damp, but there are many ways of making them both stylish and usable.

**Country comfort** (left) A welcoming mass of potted plants and a jumble of found objects creates a relaxed and cozy country feel.

**Town classic** (below) A tree with a slender trunk of sculptural potential and a single potted palm suit this city location admirably.

## Improving conditions

Basement areas are often damp. Repairing walls and correcting drainage will ensure that garden runoff and moisture never infiltrate inside. Surface water should be channeled away from the building. If your basement area has been excavated to a level where there is nothing but impervious subsoil, it is essential to provide adequate drainage for gardening. Before planting, the subsoil should be excavated to a depth of 3 ft (1 m) and filled with a layer of loose hardcore (or similar material), followed by a layer of improved topsoil in which to grow plants.

## Structural changes

Basement areas can be transformed by building in a series of slightly raised "pads." Two or three of these arranged in an overlapping pattern will create a sense of movement that will prevent the eye from wandering up surrounding walls and out of the site. Series of gentle level changes can also be used to great effect in areas between street level and a small basement entrance, as shown in the design solutions on page 128.

Color is the obvious way to bring interest to a basement area and to brighten it up if it is shady. Paint the walls, perhaps with a *trompe l'oeil*, or experiment with mirrors to add visual excitement and make the area appear larger.

## Visual anchors

Providing a feature to anchor the eye within your site will prevent it from being dominated by surrounding buildings. Whether you choose a piece of furniture, a plant, or a piece of sculpture, keep its scale large in relation to the size of the space, since tiny, delicate features will look insignificant and provide no anchor at all.

## Colored planting

Single-color planting schemes, using light tones of gold and silver, for instance, are an effective way of bringing life to a basement yard. Alternatively, you might like to rely on the shape and texture of foliage. Be wary of what you plant directly alongside a high wall, since tall plants will lean inward to reach the light.

# "... anchor the eye within your site"

**Seasonal display** (below) Shrubby and annual materials can be supplemented with bulbs for spring enjoyment. Bold, repeating pots of narcissus make an excellent example seasonal display.

**Maximizing growing potential** (bottom) Narrow stairs allow access to plants growing in a lighter and sunnier part of this basement area.

**Plants to balance structure** (opposite) Plants with strong architectural form often thrive in shade, and contrast well with surrounding structure.

# Room for design: basements

This basement consists of a sunken area lying between the street and a basement entrance. Steep steps lead down from street level to the small paved area, which is surrounded by walls.

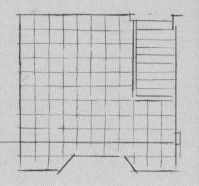

Basement entrance

### Design solution
### Version one

In this suggested solution, the area has been transformed by replacing the original steep flight of steps with a series of gentle changes in level, which make a gradual transition to street level. The shapes of the stepped levels, built-in storage space and areas of planting, and the pattern of the paving all provide a strong visual anchor, which prevents the eye from wandering up the surrounding walls or straight through the site to street level. A large piece of sculpture acts as a central focal point; areas of planting echo the shapes of the design.

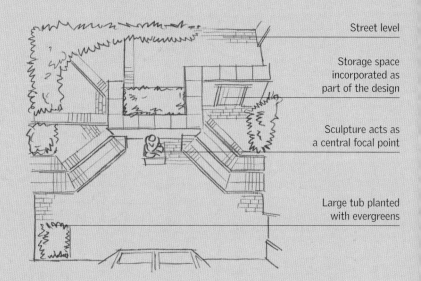

Street level

Storage space incorporated as part of the design

Sculpture acts as a central focal point

Large tub planted with evergreens

### Design solution
### Version two

Storage is often a problem in small yards. Here, a storage enclosure has been included as an integral part of the design. This acts as a visual pivot for the series of paved level changes and provides the area near the house with a measure of privacy.

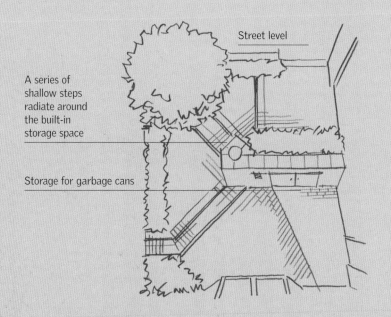

Street level

A series of shallow steps radiate around the built-in storage space

Storage for garbage cans

**Clean lines**
This deep basement has an iron staircase that is textured to minimize slipperiness in wet weather.
Large-scale lattice squares avoid a fussy effect.

# Narrow spaces

Narrow passageways and side entrances tend to be shady, drafty, and generally unappealing. More often than not, they become home to an untidy collection of garbage cans and old household bits and pieces. However, with the help of a few structural alterations and the introduction of plants as a soft overlay, they can be transformed into spaces that are pleasant to walk through and look at, both from inside and from the street.

"The **directional** pull of a **passageway** can be used to **positive** effect"

**Paving pattern** (left) Paving pattern and pots give interest to a typically stingy space at the side of a townhouse.

**Tapestry effect** (opposite) Richly patterned encaustic floor tiles set a tapestry theme, further enriched by masses of potted plants.

## Architectural solutions

Long, narrow spaces draw the eye through them, too often to an ugly endpoint—a dilapidated fence or run-down building. The directional pull of a passageway can be used to positive effect to draw attention to an eye-catching feature. A dramatic piece of sculpture, a large urn on a plinth, or *trompe l'oeil* painted on the wall at the bottom of the passage are all suitable for this.

Alternatively, the area can be given an impression of breadth by the arrangement of features or ground surface materials, used to draw the eye from side to side. Planters built across the passageway, or areas of paving across gravel, will have this effect.

## Screens and arbors

A screen can be used to break up the view down a passageway by creating a frame for various areas of interest. If filled with a solid material (glass for a view through, or painted wood to block an ugly view), it will also block uncomfortable drafts.

Tall buildings or boundary walls towering on either side of a passageway produce an unpleasant "chasm" effect, which can be reduced by erecting arbor horizontals across the area (see page 186 for more on arbors). Hanging baskets can be attached to the beams. Solid screens made of brick, concrete, or wood, projecting like buttresses from the side walls, will also help reduce the effect and can be softened by growing climbers along them.

**Fern heaven** (opposite, left) Overhead beams may slightly shade an area, but the space below is ideal for ferns.

**Focal point** (opposite, right) A mature tree trunk, here further enhanced, will always provide a focal point.

**Stepped planters** (right) Crisp design helps make this minuscule space into a little garden in its own right.

**Simple approach** (above) Fine-leaved bamboo grown in containers works well, providing form but also allowing light into the house.

**Hard and soft** (left) Monumental stone steps are softened by foliage borders.

## A soft overlay

Having used architectural solutions to solve the basic visual shortcomings of the space, use plants to soften the hard outlines of most of its structural elements. Containers or planters are indispensable, since most plants can be grown in them and they save importing quantities of soil where none exists. Since shade and drafts do not make for ideal growing conditions, you may need to choose plants that are tough. For year-round shape, select a handsome evergreen shrub, perhaps from *Pyracantha* spp. (which will tolerate full shade) or *Fatsia japonica* (which tolerates semishade). Climbers can be used to break up large areas of wall. *Parthenocissus* spp. can withstand drafts and grow in semishade, and *Hedera* spp. will survive in shade.

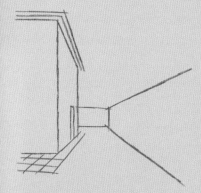

# Room for design: narrow spaces

This uninviting side entrance is transformed in three different ways in the design solutions on this page. Rather than resting in the area, the eye is drawn straight through and out of sight by the right-hand wall. The entrance is also drafty—wind funnels through the passageway from the viewpoint.

**Design solution**
**Version one**
Three brick planters built across the passageway create a sense of movement that detracts attention from the length and narrowness of the area by leading the eye, rhythmically, from side to side. Evergreen shrubs in the planters act as an effective windbreak.

**Design solution**
**Version two**
A timber screen, filled in with glass, shelters the passageway from the wind without blocking out the light. (To completely obscure an unwanted view, use brightly painted timber panels instead of glass.) Beyond the glass screen, painted brick screens echo the shape of the glass panels and a T-shaped area of paving creates a welcome sense of breadth.

**Design solution**
**Version three**
Three different surface materials have been used to break up the narrow area and give it an illusion of size. Brick paving leads the eye across the foreground to an area of gravel, and down to an area of grass.

# Steps

Though steps hardly conform to most people's idea of a garden, they provide the frustrated urban gardener with a valuable space for growing plants (in pots on the steps themselves, or either side of them), and can be styled so that they make a visually pleasing link with the home and its interior.

"A **turn** in the stairway creates an added **sense** of **movement**"

**Graceful line** (left) These steps gracefully follow the line of the bay window behind them.

**Country steps** (right) A mix of stone and brick creates a more rural feel.

**Pot lined** (below) This flight of steps is broad enough to be lined on either side with a row of matching pots.

## Styling steps

Basic structural repairs, such as replacing crumbling brickwork and broken treads, will not only improve the look of the steps but make them safer to use, as will attention to details, such as the addition of a stylish handrail and light fixtures.

New stairways should be designed so that they blend in with surrounding architecture. Use the same, or similar, materials and try to echo features. A gently curved stairway, for example, will enhance round-topped doors and arched windows.

An L-shaped return at the bottom of a stairway will make the stairway spacious and provide a spot for standing pots or sculpture without blocking the stairs. A turn in the stairway creates an added sense of movement, and the area beneath it can be used for storage.

## Plants for steps

Plants alongside steps should have bold, architectural shapes so that they balance the steps' strong structural form. Evergreen shrubs are ideal, since they provide shape and interest all year. Handrails and adjacent walls can be decorated with climbers, and colorful annuals grown in pots on the steps themselves (take care not to block the pathway). If you live on a busy street, choose plants that are resistant to polluted air.

**Grass foil** (above right) Bold ornamental grasses soften the monumental strength of these natural stone steps.

**Clever match** (right) This marblelike flight, with curving treads, actually of timber, is stained white to match the house siding.

**Simple timber** (below) A plain wooden flight, visually balanced by strong and varied foliage.

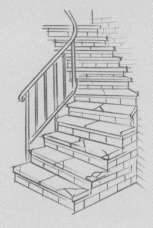

# Room for design: steps

This old, run-down flight of steps, which leads up from street level to a city home, is transformed into an inviting entrance "garden" in the three design solutions shown below. The existing steps not only look bare and uninviting but are unsafe because of the worn and cracked treads.

### Design solution
### Version one

The old steps have been redesigned and rebuilt; the L-shaped return, decorated with pots, creates a spacious look.

The rounded shapes of the planting visually echo the stone spheres

New concrete treads

Brick piers and stone spheres emphasize the rhythm of the stairway

### Design solution
### Version two

Brick piers, decorated with pale stone spheres, which match the new concrete treads, punctuate the flight of steps and lead the eye upward.

### Design solution
### Version three

The stairway has been replaced by wooden steps with a built-in cupboard. The soft shapes of the planting contrast with the crisp lines of the structure.

Stained cedar steps

Storage cupboard for garbage cans and garden tools

# Roof spaces

For city-dwellers, rooftops are particularly valuable areas that can be transformed into congenial places in which to sunbathe, entertain, and eat outside, and in which children can play (provided that there are adequate safety barriers).

"the sky overhead and a view
stretching into the distance
can be rather overwhelming."

## Creating a rooftop room

Try to create a roomlike atmosphere so that you feel you are sitting in the roof space as you would a room, rather than perching on it, since the enormity of the sky overhead and a view stretching into the distance can be rather overwhelming. Painting walls, replacing or covering the original roofing material with weatherproof flooring or lightweight paving, lighting for the evenings, and furniture will all make a roof-space more congenial.

Planting can then be used to add a refreshing touch of greenery and color that will soften the stark lines of surrounding buildings. Because roofs are exposed to the elements, permanent planting must be resilient (see page 314 for suitable plants), or given shelter from strong winds.

A convenient water supply and regular maintenance are vital to their success because the wind has a dehydrating, foliage-burning effect and container-grown plants have a limited moisture reserve.

Always consult your landlord and/or a structural engineer before using a roof or making any structural changes to it. Heavy elements are best sited over or close to direct structural support—usually the edge of the roof space.

**High-level access** (opposite) Access to this sheltered roof terrace is from the floor above, providing a marvelous viewing balcony.

**Contained** (above) Aluminum containers, double-skinned to protect plants against the heat, enclose this small deck terrace between brick chimney stacks.

**Planters** (left) The tall planters create an interesting space and help to disguise the surrounding screening.

**Furniture** Rust-colored modular seating/storage units and planters (above) harmonize to provide a sculptural element. Aluminum furniture (below) can stay out all year. Low, tough planting of grasses with *Pinus mugo* also gives wind protection.

# Room for design: roof space

The two treatments on this page show contrasting ways of transforming unused roof space. The roof is covered with an asphalt sealant and there is an unused chimney on the left-hand side. Access is through a window situated at the viewpoint. In design solution version one, this is simply replaced by a door, while in version two, a completely new access is built into the side of the pitched slate roof, which contains a new living room.

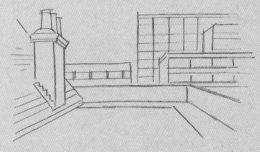

**Design solution
Version one**

The previously ignored roof space has been transformed into a bright and informal room designed for partying and relaxing in. The area in front of the chimney has been turned into a bar area.

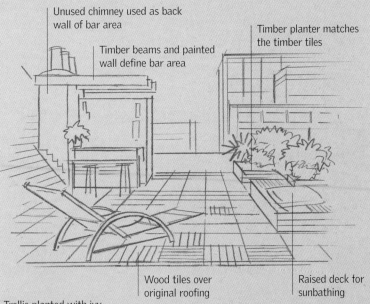

Unused chimney used as back wall of bar area

Timber beams and painted wall define bar area

Timber planter matches the timber tiles

Wood tiles over original roofing

Raised deck for sunbathing

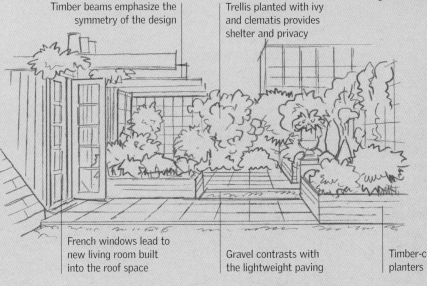

Timber beams emphasize the symmetry of the design

Trellis planted with ivy and clematis provides shelter and privacy

**Design solution
Version two**

This rooftop design is more formal and less flamboyant in style than version one, so that it works well as a visual extension to a new living room (built under the pitched roof).

French windows lead to new living room built into the roof space

Gravel contrasts with the lightweight paving

Timber-covered lightweight planters

# Balconies

A balcony, however small, can be transformed into a valuable visual extension of the living area it adjoins, to be enjoyed all year, and, though it may be dusty and windy, can be a pleasant place on which to tend a few plants and sit or entertain in the summer.

"... a valuable visual **extension** of the **living** area"

**Inviting** (above) Always a squeeze in use, a planted balcony looks very inviting from inside the house.

**Half and half** (right) Half of this roof terrace has become a conservatory, allowing just enough space for a collection of plants in pots on the balcony.

## Styling a balcony

Using the same flooring inside and out is one of the simplest and most effective ways of integrating a balcony with an adjoining room. Standing a few pots of plants on the interior flooring will strengthen the link by bringing outside in. Use the same style of furniture you have inside on the balcony, or just take a few of your usual chairs outside (this will solve the problem of storing extra furniture), and continue your interior color scheme outside by painting walls in the same or similar shades.

Lighting your balcony artificially (either from outside or inside) will enable you to extend its use on summer evenings. But whatever the time of year, sympathetic lighting will enhance a balcony after dark, making it a view in its own right or providing an interesting foreground to the city lights that lie beyond.

**Living room view** (above left) The view from inside the house is as important as usage.

**Inventive use** (above) A clean, minimal approach. This table base is a light well for the space below.

## Shade and shelter

Awnings, a large umbrella (see page 240), or roller shades like those in design solution version one (opposite) are the obvious ways to provide shade. But plants can be useful as well as decorative. Shrubs, like boxwood, or climbers, such as ivy, trained up trellises, fencing, or over railings, will provide shelter from the wind and a measure of privacy, as well as obscuring unwanted views. If you have a lot of plants, try to install a hose nearby to facilitate watering. (See page 314 for plants suitable for balconies.)

If you devise a scheme that involves structural changes, make sure you obtain any necessary permits and consult a structural engineer about the weight capacity of your balcony.

**Decorative access** (below left) Potted bamboos screen an entrance balcony. A roof overhang will cause plants to grow out toward the light, and creates a degree of privacy as well.

**Balcony link** (below) A terrace garden and an overhanging balcony are effectively linked by a relaxed plant association in a town setting.

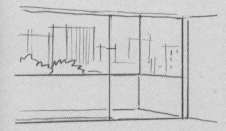

# Room for design: balcony

These three design treatments show contrasting ways of transforming this small city balcony into a congenial area in which to be and a stylish extension of the inside living area. The balcony space is surrounded by a low boundary wall, separated from a neighboring balcony by a glass panel, and divided from the adjoining living area by two sliding glass doors.

## Design solution
## Version one

The idea here is that strong, tropical pattern and color are used both inside and out, bringing light and life to the balcony and linking it with the living room it adjoins.

Awning

Yew division

## Design solution
## Version two

A yew hedge provides shade and privacy, and clipped boxwood adds year-round sculptural interest. Pots of bulbs and annuals bring a splash of seasonal color.

## Design solution
## Version three

A wall partially encloses the front of the balcony and creates two "windows." Louvered screens on runners can be slid from side to side to give different views of the balcony and skyline, creating dramatic effects, rather like those of a stage set.

# Windows

Windows make an excellent focus for decoration with paint, trellises, plants, and containers, and have a special importance for those for whom they are the only gardening space. Planning and planting a window box can be highly satisfying when the effect works!

"Choose **plants** and containers that suit the **style** of your **window** space"

**Eye-catcher** (left) Painted shutters and a colorful arrangement of petunias provide a bright eye-catcher.

**Traditional ideas** (opposite) Four selections of plant material in association with differing window treatments. Using pots and containers allows a quick change to continue winter and spring interest.

**Old-fashioned** (left) An old-fashioned begonia clashes in color with petunias and lobelia in this traditional window box, to vibrant effect.

**Using climbers** (above) Climbers can be used to frame windows. Here, fragrance is combined with color in the form of jasmine and clematis.

## Window decoration

Choose plants and containers that suit the style of your window space by looking at the color of your window frame, its surround, and the color scheme of the room inside. Ask yourself whether you want your arrangement to look most effective from outside or inside, and arrange the plants in containers that can be seen from inside so that they look pleasing when looking out through the window.

If you have no windowsill or your window opens outward, hang window boxes beneath your window, or pots around it. Alternatively, climbers can be grown from ground level and trained up and around a window. If your window is at street level and you want a measure of privacy, use plants in window boxes, or grow them from ground level to screen your room from passers-by.

# Outdoor storage

One problem in many small yards without garages is the lack of storage space for garbage cans, household bits and pieces, children's toys, and bags of potting mix, flower pots, and gardening tools.

In a large yard, such objects can usually be kept in a shed or discreetly hidden in a little-used space. In a small yard, however, where a freestanding garden shed will use up too much space, they are likely to be left in plain view unless some other type of provision for storage is made.

## Built-in storage

One solution is to build in a storage space that is an integral part of the design of your garden. Use brick, wood, or whatever material blends in with other structures in your garden. Good use can be made of awkward corners by building cupboards tailored to fit neatly into the space and designed to meet your exact requirements. The three designs opposite show ways of incorporating storage spaces into an entrance area. As part of the design of a door or gate, such practical solutions can be stylish features.

Cupboards that are to be used for storing garbage cans must be accessible and easy to clean. Items that are to be stored on a more long-term basis can be kept in less accessible places. A hollow brick bench with a removable wooden seat is ideal.

## Other solutions

An openwork screen, such as a trellis clothed with climbers, or a solid one, such as closely lashed bamboo, can be used to divide off a small area for garbage cans or a compost pile. Hedging plants make equally effective screens. Make sure that you choose an evergreen, or you will find yourself with only a seasonal rather than a permanent screen.

**Thoughtful storage** (below and opposite) Where space is short, storage is vital, but so is the subtlety of its placement. Build in your storage according to your requirements. Here are some neat, stylish examples, using a variety of cupboards and a unit with a slide-off lid.

# Room for design: storage

Here are three stylish designs for built-in storage units.

A cupboard with a lift-up lid makes for easy day-to-day use.

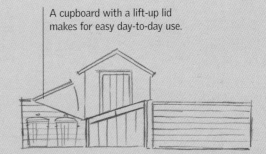

A storage cupboard designed as an extension to a gate.

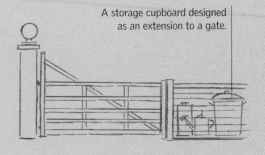

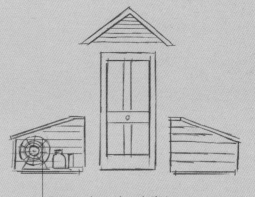

Two angular cupboards that echo the style of a door.

# structure

The materials from which your space is constructed, the way in which they are arranged, and the style of its furnishings all mold its character.

**Creative contrast** The abundant growth in the foreground contrasts with the treatment around the water feature, with repeated pyramidal hornbeams (*Carpinus betulus* 'Pyramidalis') holding the two halves together.

# Garden hardware

The structure of a small-space garden can be one of the most exciting things about it, and may well need to be if, as is often the case, its size and location make scope for planting restricted or nonexistent. The shapes of various surfaces—gravel, paving, and walling, for instance—and the characteristics of the materials from which they are made will give your garden long-lasting pattern, color, and texture. Even for those primarily interested in horticulture, the structure is important, since a mere collection of plants will become a nondescript mess if it is not contained and offset by a strong, permanent structure. The structure can be the main focus of interest in its own right, like

**Shape upon shape** Imagine the placement of the elements of this garden on a plan and you would see shape upon shape. Water provides part of the continuity, but the binding element is random paving.

the fountain and pool opposite, or it can work together with planting to create a perfect balance of hard and soft materials, like the garden featured in the photograph below. It is the structure that binds the garden, visually and physically, with its site—linking the house to the garden and the garden to the surround. The closer the link between a small space and its immediate surroundings (these often being the house and its interior), the larger that space will appear.

People need structure in their garden space, too, to provide shelter and privacy, and a practical surfacing on which to walk, place furniture, and so on. A "good" structure will suit your needs as much as those of the plants and other "furnishings" in it.

**Stepped elements**
Built blocks of various heights are juxtaposed with the entrance gate. The stepped element of the structure is carried through in the placement of the three tree ferns. Foreground sculpture provides a counterbalance.

## Structure and planting

The main structural features of this garden are the steps and waterfall, where timber has been used as a major element to reduce their impact. In addition, what could have been very heavily detailed has been beautifully softened by the planting.

### 1 Cast and capped walling

All the retaining walls have been cast in concrete, although they could equally well have been plastered concrete block. Landscape timbers have been used as a coping or capping for the walls.

### 2 Strong stepping

The same timbers are used again for the construction of the steps up the center of the garden. There is a lot going on in this garden, but its detail is so strong and simple that it works well.

**Woodpile bench** (above) Timbers appear to have been simply stacked up to create this built-in bench, while the decorative recessed leaf detail provides a refining touch.

## 4 Receding wall

The color of this rear wall makes it recede, highlighting the grassy masses in front of it. The grass is *Deschampsia cespitosa* (tufted hair grass).

## 5 Grass grid

Paving slabs with grass in between continue the soft feel of the major planting, and could be mowed with a string trimmer—a very easy item to store.

## 3 Textural waterfall

The waterfall has the same chunky appeal as the remainder of the detailing. A reservoir containing a self-circulating pump resides beneath a grid holding the pebbles above. A pipe from the pump up the rear of the wall feeds water into the top small reservoir, which then overflows to form the fall.

**Effective edging** (right) Edging a deck, especially when working with a level change, can be tricky. It has been dealt with here in a slick and simple way to stand above the pebbles beneath it.

ENCLOSURE

# Walls

One of the reasons why the traditional English country walled garden is a fascinating model for so many small-space gardeners is because their own site is hemmed in by the walls of surrounding buildings, several stories high, and of neighboring gardens. But country garden solutions are probably not the way to avoid that uncomfortable claustrophobic feeling common in town gardens. Sometimes it is necessary to build a new boundary wall or replace an old crumbling one, but more often we have to deal with the effect that "inherited" walls have on our small-garden space. The higher the boundary walls, the stronger the inclination to look up and out of the well they create, and the greater the need to counteract this tendency in your design. This can be done by building in a strong visual feature or features (in scale with the walls) that will hold the eye in the site, or by decorating the walls in various ways.

"Regard the elevation of the boundary walls as the back of a stage set"

**Wall wings** (below) Walling is the ultimate screen. These two matching screens intrigue, disguise, and provide a sculptural element.

Resist the temptation to work on a small scale just because you are dealing with a small space. In order for features to command attention, they must be in scale with the surrounding walls. Take, for example, a small garden surrounded by a 6½-ft (2-m) wall. If this measurement is used within the space, with a 6½-x-6½-ft (2-x-2-m) mass of planting and a paved area, or children's sandbox, for example, you will start to integrate the scale of the walls with that of the space enclosed and relieve the tight "banding" effect that walls can have.

The style of your internal, sculptural build-up will depend on the style of your house, and the materials from which this and the garden walls are made. Features such as a built-in bench or a small pool, built in the same material as the surrounding walls and your home, will give the garden a satisfying, integrated look.

**Gabion wall** (top) An interesting "country" effect of random planting among stone, all held within gabions of steel wire.

"Resist the temptation to work on a small scale just because you are dealing with a small space."

## Using retaining walls

Regard the elevation of the boundary walls as the back of a stage set and use low retaining walls to add interest to the set and lead the eye from the top of the boundary walls to ground level. Provided that the boundary walls are structurally sound, the area between them and the low retaining walls can be backfilled with drainage material and soil, and used for planting. However, do not, in a small space, construct retaining walls all around the perimeter of existing high walls, since this will reinforce the tight "banding" effect of the original walls, and make them appear even more dominating. Instead, break up the areas of retaining wall and use their dimensions to bring shape and pattern to the garden. It is important that walls built to retain the weight of soil are strong and that they are damp-proof. Attention to such matters will save you both time and money later.

Low walls can also be used to support paved terraces or to form a series of stepped levels. The arrangements of these should suit the shape of your garden space, and they should match the style of the architecture of adjoining buildings. It may be that a classical, symmetrical arrangement suits the proportions of your garden and the style of your home or, alternatively, the angular shape formed by the corner of your house within the yard calls for an asymmetrical arrangement.

**Colored walls** (above) Slab-colored walls are one of the three key elements of this small space, along with the sculptural form of a single tree and a water chute into a central pool.

## Shelves and panels

Collections of pots, pebbles, and shells can be arranged on shelves attached to outside walls. Before you start, make sure that the wall is strong enough to support the weight of the shelves and the objects on them. Roof-garden owners can reduce the amount of weight on the roof itself by standing container-grown plants and decorative objects on shelves attached to the main structural walls of the building it adjoins.

Sculptural panels are an effective way of decorating walls, too. An arrangement that will bring textural interest to a bland wall can be made from painted or stained wood pieces mounted on a wooden panel. Climbers, or plants that can be trailed over the top of a wall, are an ideal way of bringing color and textural interest to a bare wall, and will save you from occupying valuable ground space with plants. (See page 288 for details of some climbing plants.)

**Concrete wall frame** (top) Plastered concrete frames this impressive collection of tropical plants interspersed with sculptural features, repeated in the foreground.

**Architectural planes** (above) Here there is an architectural build-up of walls and shelving, on which pots and boulders are contrasted.

## Using climbers

Dramatic combinations can be made by painting a wall in one color and training a climber in a contrasting color over it. Panels of trellis, either covered with climbers or perhaps painted, can be used to disguise ugly walls. Over a long period of time, self-clinging climbers like ivy will begin to erode the mortar in old brick walls. However, modern mortar is more resilient, and growing climbers will have no appreciably adverse effects. Climbers, particularly evergreens, grown against any type of wall should be clipped well back, in order to prevent dead foliage or birds' nests from accumulating.

**Lattice as wall** (below) Chunky lattice detail becomes part of the garden pattern, over which to train light, delicate foliage and flower forms.

**Checker wall** (bottom) A dramatic checkerboard effect, either painted or in cast-concrete panels.

## Maintaining walls

It is very important to take care of walls, particularly old brick walls with weak mortar, which humidity and aerial roots of climbing plants may cause to crumble. Damaged brick walls need to be treated before they become unsound. Seek out expert advice to determine the cause of the problem, and take steps to repair or maintain the wall.

Outside walls can be decorated in a manner similar to inside walls—painted, tiled, hung with ceramics and shelves, and so on. Such techniques are a good way of brightening up a small-space garden while leaving maximum ground space for use, and of breaking up solid areas of surrounding wall. In warm climates, walls are often colorfully painted to relieve the sun's glare, while in duller climes the idea is to relieve the gloom. You might think that pure white is a good idea in drab conditions, but it has a tendency to turn to muddy gray when wet. Boundary walls painted in different colors or in several tones of the same color will enliven a small enclosed space and counteract its oppressiveness.

Abstract patterns of shape and color or a realistic scene can be painted on walls, too, or false shadows that will create interesting effects when overlapped by real ones. (See page 118 on the use of "special effects.")

## Focus on walls

While we happily decorate the walls inside our homes with colorful paint, hang wall panels, shelves, and collections of plates on them, and stand pieces of sculptural interest in front of them, we shy away from doing the same sort of thing outside. Using similar techniques on outside walls, where there is the added bonus of being able to enjoy the color and texture of plants that will climb up them or trail over them, will not only help create a congenial roomlike atmosphere but will also alleviate the feeling of constriction so common in small spaces surrounded by high walls. Walls can be treated like an empty canvas and decorated so that they become a focus of interest in their own right. Alternatively, they can be used as a backdrop to foreground features.

"Walls can be treated like an empty canvas and decorated"

**Plantsman's wall** (opposite, top left) A checkerboard of stone blocks built to form planting pockets. Soil is contained by wooden crosspieces.

**Snake charmer** (opposite, top right) An extraordinarily eye-catching serpentine or "crinkle-crankle" wall made from cast concrete.

**Tropical mix** (opposite, bottom left) This colorful wall for a tropical climate is made of mosaics set into concrete.

**Inside outside** (opposite, bottom right) Glass blocks, more commonly used indoors, can be employed to create a light and reflective partition outside.

# Walling choice

When choosing a walling material, you should think about how the color, texture, and unit size of different materials will suit the surrounding structures. Try to visualize the massed effect of a unit, since this can be startlingly different to looking at one example in isolation.

Brick is the most popular, given that the enormous range of colors and textures makes it possible to find one to complement almost any setting. Their small unit size makes them ideal for use in small spaces, where it is often necessary to build curved or awkwardly shaped walls. They are also excellent for building water features, seating, and other features. Engineering bricks, facing bricks, infill or common bricks, and secondhand bricks can be all used for building walls.

Engineering bricks are the hardest (throughout their structure); facing bricks are not as hard but they are stronger than infill or common brick, which must be covered with mortar (rendered) for protection against frost. Both engineering and facing brick will give a smooth, slick appearance. In contrast, second-hand or used bricks (these will be hard enough to have been reclaimed, and are therefore engineering or facing bricks) have an uneven surface because they are already weathered; these lend themselves well to walls adjacent to older buildings. Facing bricks are only weather-proofed on their finished face, so the top of a brick wall should be protected with a coping.

Concrete blocks are made from a variety of aggregates, resulting in a wide range of colors and textures. They are manufactured in larger unit sizes and are cheaper than bricks, which makes a concrete wall speedier and less costly to build than a brick one. Concrete can also be poured in situ to make a very strong wall with a smooth surface. In rural areas, local stone will probably suit surrounding buildings and landscape best. Reconstituted stone has a more regular shape, making it better suited to the urban environment.

**Dry stones** The apparent random piling of stone upon stone evokes countryside walks. Dry stone fencing must be laid by an expert.

**Poured concrete** This brusque concrete wall provides a perfect backing for the vigor of the wildflowers.

**Knapped flint and rubble** In some areas this is a traditional building material. It is often used as a facing for plain bricks.

**Colored render** The square-cut edges of this colorful rendered wall frame the curves of the sculpture, while its color echoes the planting.

**Stone flags** A more ordered version of the dry stone fence, these riven flags look even better when colonized by lichens.

**Metal lattice** This wall of angled mirrors allows formal displays to show themselves to the best effect.

**A colored background** This tinted concrete wall shows off the strong colors and shapes of the flowerheads.

**Reclaimed bricks** This wall has already done its aging. South-facing, it retains the sun's heat to give trained plants a boost.

**Tiles for decoration** An undecorated, curved flight of tiles on top of the smooth wall contrasts with the rounded shapes of the flooring cobbles. As its height increases, the smooth surface of the wall helps carry the eye upward.

# Fencing

Fencing is versatile and has many uses in the small-space garden. High panels of solid fencing can be used to create a wall-like barrier that will provide privacy and shelter, with the advantage that it is cheaper, easier to erect, and lighter than walling (thus ideal for roof-spaces and balconies). Openwork fencing, or trellis, is often used to decorate or extend the height of existing walls. Other types of fencing can be used as a boundary demarcation, which, rather than acting as a barrier, will give you a glimpse of the outside world and increase the feeling of space in your small patch. Within a small garden space, different types of fencing can be used to screen unsightly structures, provide shelter (for both people and plants), create secluded areas, frame interesting glimpses or features, or as a decorative support for climbing or trailing plants.

There are dozens of different types of fencing. Some are prefabricated, such as "larchlap" fencing or trellis, which is bought in panels. Others can be constructed, for instance chain link held in a wooden border, or bamboo

fastened to rush matting. Depending on the height and shape of a fence and the material from which it is made, the finished effect will range from crisp and architectural to natural and rustic. Your choice will depend on what kind of barrier you need as well as the color and texture of the other materials used in your garden, such as brick, concrete, wooden, or metal.

**Diamond-tipped fence**
(above) This blue-stained stockade-style boundary is a unique feature.

"...create secluded areas, frame interesting glimpses or features"

**Formal set piece**
Trellis fencing is backed here with bamboo to create a three-dimensional effect, which silhouettes a clipped standard tree.

## Decorative divisions

It is often necessary to create some sort of division between a garden space and its surroundings. You may need to divide your small front yard from the street, or decide to replace a low chain and post fence that divides your strip of garden from its neighbors with something less minimal, which will give you at least some measure of privacy. Before choosing a particular type of fence, ask yourself a few questions. Do you want to seclude your space from the outside world or do you just want some sort of attractive boundary demarcation? Or do you, for instance, wish to retain the pleasant view on one side of your garden and hide an ugly building on the other?

**Traditional cottage** (above left)
A classic cottage garden picket fence often provides an excellent foil for traditional planting.

**Bamboo behind bamboo** (above)
Bamboo rolls fixed to more robust timber verticals are fine short-term, but this type of bamboo soon deteriorates.

## Fencing all round

In our zeal to give ourselves privacy and/or shelter, we all too often box in our space with high, solid fencing, which exaggerates the limitations of its size and can make it feel claustrophobic too. There are several ways of minimizing this effect. One is to balance the area of fencing visually with a strong structural pattern within the garden, as you might if your space were surrounded by high walls. Another is to soften the outline of the fencing with bold masses of plant material. Fencing will keep pets and children in as well as defining the boundaries of your garden.

**Robust lattice-work** (top)
Interwoven metal lattice, much more robust than timber.

**Japanese-style screen** (above)
Bamboo rolls used to run vertically with lattice, to create a suitably Japanese-style effect.

There are numerous types of open fencing (chain link and trellis to name but two); choose one that complements the style of your garden space. Openwork fencing is a good support for climbing plants, which are ideal for small gardens because they take up so little ground space. They can be used to infill areas of see-through fencing to provide seasonal or year-round shelter and privacy, or grown up trellis-work to decorate a wall. Wires stretched between timber verticals make an excellent form of fencing/plant support and can easily be constructed. Fencing is much lighter than walling and thus can be used to give a balcony or roof-space privacy and shelter, without imposing too much strain on the structure. Make sure that you are not infringing any planning regulations and that the fence is well secured so that the wind does not blow it over.

## Fencing within the garden

Fencing (including railings or a metal fence) can be used within your garden space as well as around it. It can be used to hide parts of a garden you would rather not see—garbage cans, an oil tank, or a compost heap, for instance. Woven panel or close-board fencing will do the job admirably, as will open fencing covered with an evergreen climber. A small area used for eating or sunbathing in will assume a roomlike atmosphere if it is either partially or completely screened by fencing and, depending on your choice of fence, will offer privacy and shelter from the wind. Screens made from fencing can be used purely for their visual effect too, to frame a feature within the garden—a piece of sculpture, for instance—or just to create interesting shapes in their own right. Another advantage is that a glimpse through a trellis or any other type of closely spaced screen will, by blurring the outlines of what lies beyond, give the smallest of spaces an illusion of size.

**Palisade effect** (top right) Split conifer pole fencing, which creates a solid division.

**Lightweight effect** (middle right) A galvanized wire grill screen with a circular cutout.

**Diamond lattice** (bottom right) Here, lattice has been used against a solid fence and painted to match.

**Screened art** (opposite) A foil for the sculpture beyond, this steel screen has been left to rust.

# Fencing choice

Fencing should suit its purpose as much as its location. Black trellis-work, for instance, would make a sophisticated screen for an eating area, with minimal planting and chic, black furniture, whereas plain timber picket fencing would make a simple, decorative boundary between a small, country-style town garden and the street. Plastic, metal, and timber are the most common fencing materials (concrete is usually only used for fence posts). Many types of fencing are prefabricated and are assembled on site, but some such panels may be too large for your site. By designing your own fencing, you can tailor it to fit the exact dimensions of your space, and to suit the style of the rest of your garden space.

Plastic suits urban locations better than rural ones and is maintenance free. Most prefabricated, plastic fencing is low-level and serves to define a boundary rather than enclose it. Metal fencing in the form of rolls of wire mesh and chain link (sometimes covered in plastic) is ideal for curving around awkwardly shaped spaces. It can be supported by metal, concrete, or timber verticals, or fixed into a frame.

There is a style of timber fencing to suit just about every practical purpose and every location. Unless you use very expensive hardwoods, timber must be stripped of bark and then treated with a wood preservative, or sealed and then painted, to prevent decay. Timber rots if left in direct contact with the ground, so timber verticals should be placed in a metal shoe, which in turn should be set in a concrete foundation, and timber fencing panels raised slightly above the ground.

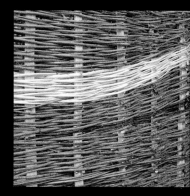

**Willow weave** Panel of woven willow for a rural setting.

**Softwood weave** Interwoven softwood horizontals need sturdy verticals and bottom edging.

**Rural paling** Open split-hazel paling fencing, for a very rural look.

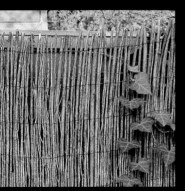

**Upright bamboo** Bamboo rolls used vertically to good effect.

**Larchlap panelling** Being solid, larchlap panels need robust verticals to stop the wind blowing them over.

**Weathered weave** Panels of interwoven hazel look more rustic the older, more weather-worn and overgrown with climbers they become.

**Traditional picket** Classic cottage-type picket paling.

**Seashore style** Sea-washed driftwood would look great in the right situation.

**Upright larchlap** Larchlap panels used so that the timbers run vertically.

# Entrances and exits

Entrances are important not just because "first impressions count" but because the only outside space that many town- and city-dwellers have is the small area between street and door—an alleyway, a path, or maybe just a doorstep.

The traditional approach to a house consists of three parts: a gate, a path (usually through a small garden), and a front door. These are usually designed together to give a stylistically unified look; the details of the gate matching those of the door, which in turn echo architectural characteristics of the house. But current urban living, with its high-rise apartments, conversions, split-levels, and the need for security, makes for unconventional and less-obvious approaches round the sides of buildings, through passageways, down steps, or through security gates. These can nevertheless be styled so that they make a satisfying transition between the street and the home. Whether the approach to your home is traditional or unconventional, you can emphasize it, brighten it, and make it welcoming too.

"emphasize it, brighten it, and make it welcoming"

**Fine detailing** (right) sculptural cast-metal doorway into a small courtyard makes an uplifting detail.

**Sense of drama** (left) This gate opens onto a winding path of complex patterns to lead the eye through the garden.

## Setting the mood

The material of your path, passageway, or entrance area; the style of your gate; the color of your door and its type of fixtures and fittings; and the tubs and pots around it should all suit the style of your home and set the mood for what lies within.

Let your choice be guided by the architectural style of your home. Try to echo its characteristics, in the shape, color, materials, or decorative patterning of your door or gate. There are as many types of gate as there are architectural styles, ranging from ornate late 19th-century metal gates to cottage picket gates and ranch-style gates. Echoing the style of a front door in particular (its shape, color, material) in that of a gate will visually link the two and unify the space between them.

Look too at the structure your door or gate pierces. A slick brick wall, for instance, would be best suited to a crisp, modern design in smooth painted wood, or metal, whereas a textured stone wall would be complemented by a more rustic design in natural wood. A front door or gate should also suit the character of the rest of the street, since they are very much part of the whole community.

**Rustic scene** (top left) The gate and fence structure complements the stone wall and reduces the sense of a barrier between one side and the other.

**Country style** (above) Painting the standard country garden-style picket fence and gate in a soft gray helps to accentuate the colors of the planting.

**Inviting entrance** (below) Framing the view into the garden, this ornate gate also acts as a support for a climbing plant, creating a mood before you enter.

**Unified approach** (bottom right) Crisp-looking iron gates complement the plain walls containing this entrance space. The lights have been considered as part of the overall concept and not as later additions.

## Gates for privacy and security

Many people who live in urban areas are becoming increasingly security conscious and therefore have front gates specifically designed for that function, which are high, robust, and sometimes controlled from within the home. This type of gate is usually made from metal rather than wood and, when well-designed and in keeping with the surroundings, can be attractive as well as functional. Privacy too is often sought by those who live on busy streets. In conjunction with a high wall or close-board fencing, a solid or louvered gate (made from wood or metal) can be used to enclose the area between street and home, giving complete privacy from passers-by. Small areas enclosed like this, paved or perhaps surfaced with gravel and furnished with benches and a few plants in containers, can assume a pleasant, courtyard quality, making the entrance to the home a congenial and private space for sitting outside and in which children can safely play.

Although other types of gate (low wooden gates, iron railing gates, and slatted gates) can prevent small children and pets from getting out, they are primarily a decorative break in a boundary rather than a barrier against intrusion, both physical and visual. They mark an entrance and give both the passer-by and the person within a glimpse of the other side. Low gates, by creating a break in a solid boundary wall, for instance, have the advantage of making a confined space seem larger and preventing it from appearing boxed in.

## The approach

Although the approach to your home—be it a regular-shaped space with a path, some winding steps, or a narrow passageway—should be safe and practical, you should also aim to make it a stylish extension of your home. If such an area is your only outside space, you will undoubtedly wish to make the most of it. (See pages 130 and 136 respectively for design ideas for narrow spaces and for steps.)

A narrow path leading straight through a small area between the street and a front door will, by dividing it up, make it appear smaller. Instead, pave a small entrance area in an overall pattern (see p.196 for the visual effect of different paving patterns) or lay it with gravel, since this will give it a homogeneous look and make it appear larger. Where the paving's primary purpose is to provide a service pathway, however, ensure that slippery surfaces, planting, and changes of level are kept to a minimum. Materials with textured surfaces, such as brick, give a better foothold than smooth ones, such as concrete. Often, the area directly between the street and home has to be used for parking and therefore is in effect a driveway. Make sure that access for cars is free of obstacles or narrow gates that make driving in and out a test of nerves. The ground surface should have drainage in the form of gulleys leading to a land drain or culvert, or a fall into the surrounding ground, so that water used for washing your car will drain away.

**Naturally ornate** (left) Stones of various sizes create a rural-style pathway that is easy to look at, but probably slightly less easy underfoot.

## Doors and doorsteps

Doors, whether they are on the street or set back from it, can be decorated so that they are welcoming and set the mood for what lies behind them. Make the most of painted color, either on the door itself or to accentuate moldings or other architectural features. The size of a doorstep can be increased by building a small plinth either side of it, or by extending it forward. A well-placed pot or piece of sculpture on the doorstep, or a decorative wreath hanging from the door, will make an entrance both obvious and welcoming to visitors. If your door is on the street, make sure that any decorative items are firmly attached, since weight alone is no deterrent to anyone determined to make it his own. A pergola-type structure attached at one end to the wall around a door and supported at the other by free-standing verticals is a good way of leading visitors to entrances that are less obviously situated. (Examples of pergolas are featured in the following section.)

Trash cans often have to be kept near a front door for practical reasons. If there is room, they can be hidden in a built-in cabinet (made from brick, wood, or whatever material most suits the style of your house), perhaps with a plant container that is integral to the design. Alternatively, they can be hidden behind an evergreen shrub, or a trellis-work screen covered with an evergreen climber; Common ivy, *Hedera helix* 'Goldheart', for example, would do this most effectively.

It becomes obvious when seeking someone's home, particularly from behind a driving wheel at night, how many houses have ineffective and unhelpful lights and signs, making it difficult ot find them at all. Illuminating your front door and the number or name of your home will make it easier for visitors to find you and safer if you are returning home late at night. Position the source of light so that its beam shines upward to create a warm, subtle glow, rather than a harsh, dark shadow created by a light shining downward from a high position. (See page 236 for more on lighting effects.) Choose a light fitting that suits the style of your home—however charming itself, an "old-world" carriage lamp can ruin the effect of a slick, modern entrance.

**Pleasing symmetry** (right) Simple brickwork steps and basket-weave brick paving provide a matching entrance to the brickwork of the house.

# Pergolas

Perhaps the image of the pergola that springs most readily to mind is that of a vine-entwined structure used in sunny Mediterranean climates to create shade and form a covered transition between buildings. Pergolas have many other practical and visual uses in a small space—they can form a semi-covered room or a plant-covered arbor, or be used to strengthen some aspect of a garden's design.

Pergolas that lead from one space to another are what I call dynamic or directional pergolas. In contrast, those that cover a wider area, and define a space rather than lead through it, are static in nature.

### Directional pergolas

Directional pergolas can be free-standing or connected to a building. The free-standing type draws the eye down its length, thereby shortening the foreground perspective. There are situations where this is desirable, for instance where a pergola leads the eye to and frames a view or an entrance, or where it is constructed over a path. However, the ground on either side of directional pergolas tends to become merely the "leftovers" in small spaces. Directional pergolas attached to the side of a building create a colonnade effect and are useful for covering an entrance or keeping the sun from rooms inside. If, in a hot climate, the pergola's structure and planting alone do not provide enough shade, a roller blind can be attached to the top and pulled across. Alternatively, split and rattan cane blinds can be used to fill in the gaps between the horizontals, which will also create interesting shadows on the ground. In colder climates, blinds are not usually necessary because the spreading, foliage of annual climbers is enough to soften the sun's effect, while in winter, the stark pergola frame allows the light in.

**Fruit tree canopy** (above) Interconnected simple metal hoops are ideal as a framework for training fruit trees.

## Static pergolas

Static pergolas—those that do not lead in one direction but cover a larger area, such as a terrace, or even the entire garden—are a good way of extending the mood of an interior and creating, visually at least, an additional room outside. By providing a ceiling (in the form of the pergola's horizontals), it is possible to create the feeling of being in a room outside, thus weakening the barriers between inside and outside and increasing the overall feeling of space. Such static pergolas are rarely free-standing structures, with uprights at both ends of the horizontals. In a small space, there is certainly not enough room for this. Rather, the horizontals are connected to a wall at one end, and sail outward to meet the verticals that rise from the edge of the total covered space. Or uprights may not be required at all, the horizontals simply bridging the gap between two walls, for instance two boundary walls, or a house wall and a boundary wall.

## Pergolas on roofs

Roof gardens are often rather exposed, not only to the wind and the great expanse of sky above but to surrounding buildings, and consequently they are not always very congenial. A pergola constructed on a roof will give the space a sheltered feel and, if covered with tough climbing plants, will protect against sun and wind. It is important to check the strength of a roof before constructing a pergola, since its weight can be considerable (you may need planning permission too). Metal frames are lighter than wooden ones, and if there are walls either side of the roof area, metal wires or rope can be used.

## "Pergolas make wonderful hosts to climbing plants"

## Planting

Pergolas, whether free-standing or adjoining a building, make wonderful hosts to climbing plants—one of the most attractive aspects of a plant-covered pergola is the quality of dappled light that filters through the foliage. Plant material will soften the overall effect of the structure and help provide shade and privacy, the latter being of great benefit in towns and cities where gardens are so often overlooked. Growing plants vertically is also an excellent way of saving space at ground level. Remember, however, to consider the weight of any envisaged planting in relation to the strength of the pergola, particularly if you wish to train plants along wires or rope. Bear in mind too the density of the plant's foliage and the length of time it is in leaf, since this will affect the amount of shade provided. Evergreen climbers, for instance, may create too much shade in the winter months when maximum light is needed.

## Pergolas for proportion

In many urban areas, where garden spaces are not in scale with surrounding buildings, a pergola's horizontals can be used to lower the height of the space and create an esthetically pleasing and proportioned area that is comfortable and inviting. If the style of the pergola suits the architecture around it, it will link the space covered more closely with its surroundings. One of the most useful facets of any sort of pergola is that its horizontals, or the shadows cast by them, can provide a useful visual framework within which to work when designing the rest of the garden. The shapes created by the horizontals can be echoed in similarly proportioned areas of paving, gravel, and planting. This will help create the integrated, consistent look that is so visually satisfactory in a small-space garden.

**Color contrast** (opposite top left) For much of the growing season, the red of this climbing rose will contrast with the eggshell blue of this simple timber pergola.

**Room divider** (opposite top right) A simple metal overhead to take a vine frames the sunbathing terrace, with a dining area beyond.

**Fragrant room** (right) The width of this pergola, clothed in fragrant *Trachelospermum jasminoides*, suggests a room in its own right.

## Pergola choice

It is important that the pergola as a whole should be in keeping with the mood and style of the buildings around it. As shown in the photographs in this section, materials can be treated in different ways to create very individual looks. A pergola's horizontals can be made in varying dimensions and from a wide range of materials, depending on how much light you want to have from above and your desired look. The verticals must be made from a material strong enough to support the weight of the horizontals. Visually speaking, however, horizontals should be considerably heavier than uprights.

Wood is the most common material for pergolas. Softwood can be used planed or sawn, depending on whether you want a smooth or textured surface. Hardwood is much more expensive, but it is more durable. Any type of wood can be painted, stained, or just treated with a wood preservative. The ends of the pergola horizontals can be shaped to echo architectural features. Metal is also suitable for constructing pergolas. It is lighter than wooden logs and does not create such an impression of division. To create a pergola that is lighter still, use tensioned wire or brightly colored chandler's rope as the horizontals, and suspend them between two walls.

**Planting in scale** A massive structure in metal could take a bolder leaf form to be in scale.

**Woven roof** This natural cover protects from the elements but without creating too dark a space.

**Contemporary** This modern form provides support for the plants but also allows plenty of light through.

"...**materials** can be treated in **different** ways to create very **individual** looks."

GROUND PATTERN

# Paving

The surface material you have outside should suit your garden as much as the flooring you have inside your home suits its various rooms and, just like choosing an interior flooring, you should consider the style, cost, and practical suitability of different materials. Paving, in all its various forms, is one of the most useful of surfaces outside. It provides a firm surface for furniture, pots, and other features, requires little maintenance, and can act either as a neutral backdrop or as a feature in its own right.

## Paving designs

Your first consideration, whatever your final choice of paving material, should be to decide on a paving design, by which I mean the overall combination of shapes as well as the position of any individual paving units within these. It is important to decide on this early, since different paving designs, from a uniform sheet of material on one hand to intricate interlocking units on the other, will radically alter the look of a space. Broadly speaking, paving patterns can be divided into those that are static and those that are dynamic. Static paving patterns hold the eye within the site, or one part of it, while dynamic paving patterns lead the eye through it. Some paving patterns have the effect of visually dividing up a space into individual mini rooms; others, usually those that are very densely patterned, hold the eye in one spot. A very bland pattern, or none at all, will emphasize the overall shape of the area paved and act as a neutral backdrop to other aspects of the garden's design.

**Fast track** (above) A simple directional run of coursed brick paving. Bricks used running across the width of the path would slow the pace down.

**Poured concrete pattern** (left) The contrasting panels within this paving circle were formed by varying poured concrete mixes.

## Dynamic paving patterns

In contrast, dynamic paving patterns create a sense of movement and visual pull. In a conventional, comparatively large garden space, there might be traditional pathways of hard surfacing through lawn and planting. These strong lines always lead the eye and are dynamic. In the small garden, where an area of paving might cover the entire space available, you can only create a dynamic scheme through the arrangement of a pattern within the paving, or by aligning areas that flow one to another so that they lead the eye.

Linear paving patterns will work where the visual pull has a satisfying conclusion—for instance, a pleasing view or a sculptural feature—or has a practical function, like a path leading to a front door. A static surface design is usually preferable when paving an enclosed space with no one point of focus, such as a terrace used for meals outside. Whether you choose a static or dynamic paving design, you will increase the apparent dimensions of a small space by having a simple paving pattern and scaling up the other features. Conversely, a heavily patterned arrangement will create a "busy" effect and emphasize its smallness.

**Pebble swirls** (below) A creative pebble arrangement creates drama, but may be too busy for a small space.

**Static squares** (bottom left) An ordered layout of bricks and pebbles also provides a lot of visual interest.

"The paving you **choose** will depend on the **style** of the enclosure."

**Calming combination** (opposite) This benign paving combination of squared stone slabs contrasted with granite pavers is ideal for a small space.

# Paving designs

These layouts show how paving patterns and the arrangement of the paving units can create very different effects within a small space.

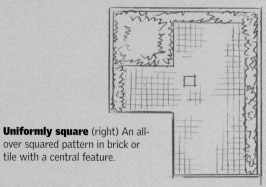

**Uniformly square** (right) An all-over squared pattern in brick or tile with a central feature.

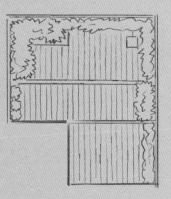

**Dynamic horizontals** (left) An even pattern of brick punctuated by horizontal lines of slate or granite pavers, or even stone. The feature becomes incidental in this design.

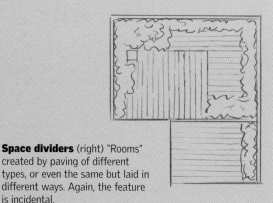

**Space dividers** (right) "Rooms" created by paving of different types, or even the same but laid in different ways. Again, the feature is incidental.

## Focus on paving

The type of paving material you choose will depend on the mood and style of the enclosure, and the materials that are available locally. Take into account the texture as well as the color of different paving materials before making your choice. The mood of a brick house, for example, with some brick walls and wooden fencing in the garden, would probably be best sustained by brick paving or or deck lumber. Stone paving, in this instance, would be less suitable, since it would probably fight with the brick, and the use of a third material would make the overall design too busy. Conversely, a space adjacent to a stone building, with stone boundary walls, probably calls for the use of wood and more stone (or concrete slabs of a similar aggregate) as the ground surface, since brick or tiles would be visually too weak.

**Paving styles** (clockwise from top left) Modern black tiles, squared stone paving, random stone slabs, granite pavers with stone surround.

# Paving choice

Natural, local paving materials are usually the most practical and suited to the environment. In rural areas, this is likely to be local stone. However, in urban areas, where there is unlikely to be a common natural building material, concrete and brick are the most universal building media. There are numerous forms of precast concrete paving, ranging from those resembling clay pavers, through slabs of varying shapes and thicknesses, to pieces the size of railroad ties. Generally, the plainer and more subdued, the better—a single virulent, heavily textured paver can look dramatic, but in a mass will be disastrous. Concrete can be laid in situ, and then brushed to expose its aggregate before it sets. As well as brick pavers, specially manufactured for paving, building bricks can be used, though the latter are softer than the former and tend to crumble. These and other small units, such as granite pavers and cobblestones, are ideal for paving small and even awkwardly shaped areas.

Consider all the surfacing materials at your disposal as a palette from which you can choose to contrast and complement the various structures of your garden. Paving an area in the same material as the surrounding walls is a good way of giving a small space a unified look and binding together the various elements of its design. Bear in mind practical considerations, too. Some materials, such as certain smooth, precast pavers, become slippery in rain and snow; others, like brick, give a good foothold.

**Creative concrete** Here, concrete has been "pressed" to look like granite.

**Random paving** "Designed" random paving using stone slabs.

**Nature's pattern** An amusing pattern of cast concrete mollusk shells.

**Brick road** A simple arrangement of coursed brick pavers.

**Concrete checkerboard** A classic checkerboard design in contrasting colors of precast concrete.

**Herringbone** The classic herringbone pattern in gray brick.

**Stone and gravel** Random stone paving and gravel set in concrete.

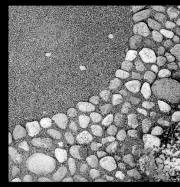

**Large stones and gravel** Large gray stones are contrasted with fine multicolor gravel, which helps to limit the number of weeds.

**Pebbles and gravel** Pebbles are here set in concrete to form edging.

# Soft surfacing

Gravel and other "soft" surfacing materials, such as pebbles and bark chips, are practical, versatile, and visually pleasing. They are cheaper and easier to lay than hard-surfacing materials such as concrete and stone, and make an ideal textural transition, being softer than paving and harder than grass or ground-cover planting.

Gravel and pebbles can be laid loose, and this is the ideal way of surfacing tight spaces that are too awkward to pave. There is one drawback, however, and this is that they are rather difficult and somewhat noisy to walk on, but this can act as a deterrent to burglars. Loose gravel and pebbles are also ideal for laying in places where little will grow and paving would be impractical—for instance, through and under trees. Leaves can be raked or blown off to leave the surface looking neat.

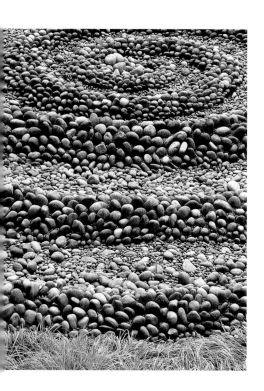

### Semi-hard surface

Gravel that has been rolled into a compressed layer of binding gravel (this is unwashed and retains a clay constituent) forms a semi-hard surface. Treated in this way, it is a perfect surface to have alongside a paved terrace area, onto which people can overflow at parties, and being porous, it can absorb an overflow of water, too. In small urban spaces, a very crisp, neat look can be obtained by using gravel instead of small areas of grass, which require considerably more maintenance, do not wear as well, and often look tired throughout the winter. Gravel that is to be used in this way should be contained by brick edging or some other hard surface.

"the ideal way of surfacing
tight spaces"

**Pebble sculpture** (above left) Small pebbles have been shaped to provide an interesting step sculpture in stones.

**Stone textures** (opposite) Brick edging is used to retain a path made from large, flat pebbles.

## Planting in soft surfaces

Shrubs, shorter herbs, seasonal bulbs, and perennials grow happily through gravel and smallish pebbles in a layer no more than 4 in (10 cm) deep. The binding layer acts as a mulch and is an ideal medium in which seeds can germinate. After all, scree gardens are composed mainly of gravel in well-drained layers—the natural medium for growing alpine plants. Planting in areas of gravel instead of bare soil confined to beds will help create a random, relaxed look, by visually binding planted areas more naturally with those of a paved area or neighboring pathway. This will also increase the apparent size of a small space, since the fewer ground divisions there are, the less cramped it will appear.

**Contrasting combinations** These pictures show the range of textural and color combinations that can be achieved when using different types of surfacing, stones, and plantings.

## Textural combinations

Japanese gardeners have used gravel as a ground surfacing for centuries, raking it into abstract patterns that simulate maritime eddies and currents swirling around islands of rock and moss. This is a technique that can be copied in small spaces, to great effect. However, it does call for regular, if not daily, care, because every shower of rain and every footprint erodes the pattern. Just as effective, and considerably less time-consuming, is the combination of unraked gravel or pebbles with boulders and rocks. This is a good way of giving a small garden an interesting abstract look. Quarried rocks are usually angular, but rounded boulders are sometimes produced during the grading process of washed stone.

# Gravel designs

The 17th-century French and Italians also used gravel between the areas of boxwood hedging in formally patterned parterres. Gravel can be put to the same formal use in small spaces, too, and can be used in conjunction with well-defined areas of planting to create a geometric pattern. Different colors and sizes of gravel can be used to create patterns, varying from a formal checkerboard effect to looser, more abstract shapes. The two drawings below show contrasting gravel designs suitable for a small-space garden. Brick or thin strips of wood or aluminum should be used to divide up the gravel; the former can be treated as part of the design. As well as being an effective way of decorating ground-level spaces, patterned gravel is a useful medium for covering a roof that is looked down on, or bringing interest to a dark well in which plants are unable to flourish.

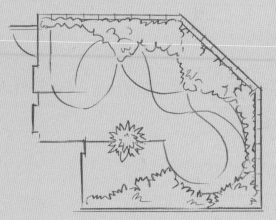

**Interwoven colors** (right) You can interweave areas of different-colored gravels to form a flowing abstract design.

**Checkerboard** (opposite top) A gravel checkerboard effect created with wooden divisions and low-growing, compact *Acaena* and *Sedum* spp.

**Succulent patterning** (opposite bottom) *Sedum* spp. making an interesting pattern among coarse gravel, suitable for a very shallow planting location.

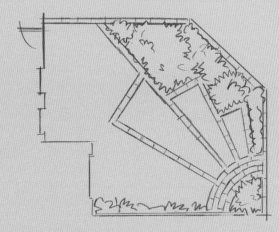

**Radiating brick ribs** (left) A bolder geometry in paving materials in conjunction with gravels.

# Soft surfacing choice

Many different looks can be created depending on the color and gauge of gravel or pebble chosen. Gravel consists of natural rock chippings, so potentially there are as many different sorts of gravel as there are types of rock. The choice ranges from white and creamy beige to gray, red, brown, and black. The range of colors of river-washed pebbles or dredged pebbles,, both of which have been rounded by the action of water, is not quite as extensive. Gravel and pebbles of any size suit just about all locations, but bear in mind that it tends to be swept up when snow is being cleared and a pale gravel can produce a lot of glare in open areas that are exposed to harsh sunlight. Pebbles are more suitable for children to play on because, unlike gravel, they have no sharp edges.

The least expensive type of soft surfacing will probably be that produced from rock native to your area. In mountainous areas, this is likely to be quarried chippings, while in areas near the sea or a large river, it may well be pebbles. In urban areas, gravel will have been imported from rural areas, so costs vary. Gravel, pebbles, and bark can be used in conjunction with hard materials. Panels of gravel within an area paved in brick or concrete will soften the overall effect and introduce a satisfying textural contrast.

When laid next to a uniformly hard surface, such as concrete paving, gravel does not need an edging. However, if it is laid next to grass or a planted area, it will need to be contained if you do not intend the two to merge. Wood, brick, or concrete can be used for edging. Choose whichever edging best suits the overall look of your garden or some of its detailing, for instance the style of a wall coping.

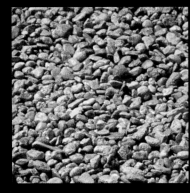

**Pebbles** Washed pebbles is perhaps the most commonly used type of soft surfacing for paths and driveways.

**White gravel** This stone gravel can make quite an impact, but can cause glare in bright sunlight.

**Coarse stones** Large slate pieces have been used here with coarse gravel for a natural look.

**In the red** Gravel is available in many colors and a red type has been used here to match the border edging.

**Shades of gray** Gray gravel is increasingly popular for soft surfacing, and can be extremely effective when contrasted with natural fibers and textures in the garden, such as this basket-weave seat.

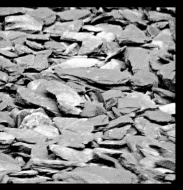

**Slate path** A decorative path made from large gray slates can be used in contrast with planting, but it is difficult to walk on.

**Wood strips** These pale wood strips look effective when placed among the grasses, but can be slippery when wet.

**Bark mulch** Bark pieces create a soft, natural-looking carpet that keeps the weeds in check.

**Perfect on roofs** (below) Deck lumber makes ideal surfacing for a roof garden, used here in conjunction with raised beds.

**Wooden path** (below right) Deck lumber used at ground level as an edging and a path to a planting. This can become slippery in winter.

"The deck really comes into its own when used in conjunction with a property on a hillside"

# Decks

Decks, which have been common in the United States and in many European countries for years (and have recently become overused on British television makeover shows), are a design option to be given careful consideration. The step between a deck and a wooden balcony is only a small one, and it might be a way to create a garden where otherwise there is no usable space. It can be tied to a building or it can be used as a freestanding surfacing material.

**Falling site drama** (opposite) Broad planes of deck lumber above a pool look clean and crisp, if potentially a little dangerous.

## The uses of decks

The deck really comes into its own when used in conjunction with a property on a hillside, where, raised on posts, it can be employed to create a level platform on the side of the building facing down the slope. The deck makes the transition out from the elevated first floor, and steps from the deck lead to ground level. This type of deck is often the only feasible way of creating a level space outside the house.

Traditionally, in the United States, older houses were built so that the living area was above ground level, leaving space beneath for a basement or cellar. Similarly, many split-level houses built today have their main living areas above ground level. In both cases, the deck is a way of extending the upper level to create a usable outside room. In the United States and Europe, low-level decks are often built instead of brick or stone terraces. This is because lumber is relatively inexpensive and suits the character of the houses, which often have wood siding or shingled roofs. Low-level decking can give a small space a pleasing, unified look when used in conjunction with wooden fencing. It need not be used to cover the whole area. Interesting patterns and satisfying textural contrasts can be created by combining small areas of deck with stone or concrete paving. Wood is also a pleasing surface to have alongside water, around a swimming pool or a small water feature. Deck lumber also makes an ideal surfacing for city roof gardens. Square wooden panels, in dimensions similar to paving slabs, can be clamped together to provide a sympathetic flooring that is not as heavy as concrete or brick.

The panels should be laid on a timber base above the roof finish, so that water can drain to an outlet. Ideally, decks should be made of a hardwood that needs no preservative treatment. Softwood, which is not as hardy, must not only be planed to prevent splintering but needs preservative treatment and becomes slippery to walk on in wet or icy weather.

**Nonslip** (opposite, top left) The boards of this deck have been grooved to reduce slipperiness in wet weather.

**Versatile** (opposite, top right) One advantage of a deck is that it can be used over tree roots and raised above ground level, even around a tree trunk, as long as it is altered as the girth of the tree widens.

**Circular boardwalk** (opposite, bottom) A boardwalk effect over a damp area, allowing a clear pool of water at the center.

# Steps

Not only are many small gardens in locations where they can only be reached by steps, but for some, a flight of steps *is* the garden. As well as enabling you to get from A to B, steps can be decorated so that they are a stylish addition to your garden, or a mini garden in their own right.

"...treat **steps** as a **sculptural** feature"

**Steps through grasses** (top)
The bulk of these irregular steps is softened by side planting of ornamental grasses.

**Garden two-step** (right) Grass terraces step at half the rate of an adjoining task-lit staircase in cast concrete.

**Granite-sett piece** (below)
Decorative curving steps in granite setts become a feature in their own right.

**Topiary lift** Clipped box balls transform this metal staircase with open risers.

## Decorating and building steps

Pots and containers are a simple and effective way of decorating steps and, if planted, of integrating the soft forms of flowers and foliage with the hard ones of structure. Painting steps or adjacent walls in a colour that tones in well with surrounding structures will give dowdy steps a new lease of life. A handrail can be a stylish and practical addition to service steps, particularly those that are steep. Good lighting will make steps a pleasure to look at, and safer at night. As well as constructing new access steps or replacing old ones, you may wish to build a shallow run of steps, as opposed to broader stepped changes of level, within your garden to give it a sense of movement and sculptural interest that will make it appear larger than it really is. Very different effects can be created according to the overall shape of the steps and the angle at which they lie in relation to surrounding structures. The three designs on the right are suitable for service steps (leading up to a front door, for instance) and steps within a small garden space.

# Steps designs

The steps in these plans are just as suitable for entrance steps as for linking changes of level in a small space. Each set of steps lies at a different angle, giving them added sculptural interest.

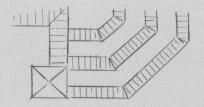

Steps that turn 45 degrees give a sense of lateral movement.

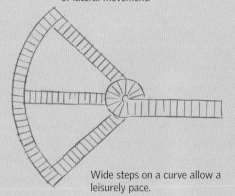

Wide steps on a curve allow a leisurely pace.

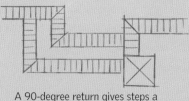

A 90-degree return gives steps a spacious feel.

**Simply ideal** (left) A minimal metal staircase is ideal for a restricted space.

**Metal and timber** (opposite left) An aluminium staircase with decking treads.

**Trad treads** (opposite right) A flight of brick steps creates a cottage-garden feel.

## Step dimensions and materials

The ideal dimensions for a set of service steps are a maximum height of 20cm (8in) and a tread width of 50cm (20in); these will give a gentle pace. Steps that take a curved or zig-zag route may need wider treads, encouraging an even more leisurely pace. Steps built in the same or a similar material as surrounding structures will blend in well and become a pleasing part of the structural pattern of a garden or building. However, safety must be considered when building service steps. Stone and timber, for instance, become very slippery after rain and frost, whereas textured materials, such as old stock brick, or a smooth material, such as concrete, infilled with a rougher material, such as stone, will give a better foothold. Do not introduce plants into the pattern of service steps, since this will make them unsafe at night and in the wet.

## "Inherited" steps

When spacious old houses or apartment blocks are converted into smaller units, steps originally designed for use as a back staircase, or a fire escape, sometimes become used as the main entrance. Conversely, grand old steps can become the route to a small apartment. An old metal staircase can be given a new lease of life with a lick of fresh paint or partially concealed with a climber. The width of grand steps can be reduced by removing some of the horizontal tread on either side, and introducing plant material in its place. When large gardens are divided up, steps that once led from one area to another can be inherited by the owner of a smaller patch, for whom they serve no practical purpose. These can be integrated into the overall design by being treated as a sculptural feature, which could be a focal point for the pattern of planting, or informal seating.

# Water

Water has a compelling quality and can bring light and life to the most limited of spaces. It is both versatile and predictable (the latter being something that plants are not), and lends itself to being contained within an architectural setting. An area of water, however styled, should be treated as an integral part of the garden's pattern, and its dimensions should be considered in relation to the height of surrounding boundaries.

**Light tray** (opposite) Even the smallest area of water can bring light down into a dark little space.

**Sound sense** (above) The sound of falling water can be soothing. However, in a restricted space it can also be loud – but better than traffic noise in town.

**Exotic vegetation** (above right) A small pond need only be warmed slightly, in northern climates, to allow such exotic foliage.

"If used properly, it will always be **eye-catching** or even **mesmerizing.**"

## Creative uses of water

Obviously, space will inhibit the quantity of water that can be included in a small garden. However, water can easily be incorporated into some sort of feature, and if ground space is very limited, it need not necessarily be one that is horizontal, for what immediately springs to my mind is the use of falling water. The effects you can achieve range from the merest trickle from a wall spout to a vertical wall of water. Though water can be cold and depressing, if used properly, it will always be eye-catching or even mesmerizing. A very significant factor that few consider is that the running, splashing, or trickling of flowing water, as well as being visually pleasing, can help to block out urban noise. On a hot day, the sight and sound of gently running water will have a cooling effect too. An area of still water at ground level in a garden creates a mirrored setting for surrounding features. A dark internal lining at the bottom of a pool of water will intensify reflections further, whereas a light-coloured glazed tile finish will reduce them. The latter treatment will tempt you to look into the water's depths, rather than its surface, adding yet another dimension to your garden space. Sunlight playing on the surface of still water produces a Hockney-like, cellular pattern and, if near a building, a reflection rather like light dancing on a ceiling.

**Simple sounds** (above) This multi-level water feature creates visual interest in its austere setting as well as a pleasant sound.

**Hydrangeas through water** (right) My favourite hydrangeas look simply magical through a curtain of falling water.

Flat planes of water can also act as a foil for planting, either in the water or adjacent to it, such as reeds and water lilies or overhanging blossoms. This is a way of linking part of your garden's ground pattern to three-dimensional plant forms. (See page 336 for plants suitable for growing in and around water.) If plants are used in association with moving water, a fountain or water splash, for instance, the relationship between structure and planting becomes more vibrant. Planes of water can be contained at different heights to create a visual relationship between the ground plan and the boundary. The focus of interest can be water flowing from one plane to another, or the "New York plaza" effect can be created, obviously on a small scale, by allowing it to form a waterfall down a wall.

Water can also be used as sculptural decoration within a basic layout, rather than as an integral part of the garden's structure. Because water has such a compelling quality, it is important that a water feature intended as decoration is contained within a strong garden plan to prevent it from dominating the entire scene. Water can be used as sculptural decoration in the form of a wall splash or alternatively in a dynamic arrangement of water-filled containers, either free-standing or interconnected.

**Floating slabs** (left) Stepping slabs across water need to be expertly constructed on plinths, so that each slab appears to float.

**Lily pond** This interesting squared pond is softened by the planting, surrounding grass and water lilies.

**Glass aqueduct** An ingenious glass rill, cut to send water pouring from a higher pool to a lower one.

## Decorative pools

Natural-looking pools of water usually appear out of character in tight urban spaces. However, though I have a personal dislike for the Japanese water garden out of its natural habitat, its rather mannered approach to wildness is more sympathetic to urban locations than the soft-edged garden pond, which only suits truly rural settings. In the main, unless extremely well-designed and crafted, the simpler the use of water in a small space, the more effective it will be. A tiny courtyard in the South of France comes to mind, in which there is a shallow pool, with a pattern of fish modelled in the tiles that line it – so simple, but constantly compelling. The water must be sparkling clean for this sort of effect, and this means excellent maintenance. There are many water-cleaning devices on the market, of varying sophistication – their installation requires specialist advice.

## Water to relax and exercise in

"Lap" pools are becoming more and more popular with the health conscious. These are areas of water designed for swimming laps in, and need not be more than 3m (10ft) in width, but should be no shorter than 7m (23ft) in length. It is just about possible to incorporate a lap pool of the minimum dimensions in a small garden, though little space will be left for anything else. Any type of swimming pool should work within a scaled layout. Frequently, the relationship between pool shape and size and the rest of the garden is ill-considered. Pear-shaped or kidney-shaped pools, so beloved by their manufacturers, are often fitted into an angular space, with the result that the areas left around them look awkward, both in relation to the pool itself and to the remainder of the garden site. A plunge pool (a pool large enough to immerse the body in) is a much smaller alternative. If fitted with a wave machine, it can provide a force of water against which to swim and exercise, and also make a natural focal point for social occasions in the summer months. Even smaller in scale are the jacuzzi and the hot tub (or even a combination of the two), which can be included in a sheltered space. If they are close to the house, they can be used in the winter. Immersing yourself in warm water with only your head in sub-zero temperatures can be a stimulating, not to say bizarre, experience.

It is essential when having warm water outside to have some sort of cover to conserve the heat so expensively generated and to keep it clean.

**Step-in water** (top and above) A hot tub or a plunge pool will fit the tiniest of garden spaces, becoming both a focal and a talking point!

**Brimming disc** (opposite) Not only does this brimming disc pool reflect, but it is also wildlife friendly, being approachable to birds and allowing tadpoles to escape as they mature.

FURNISHINGS

# Pots and containers

Pots and containers are an invaluable ingredient for furnishing and adding to the style of your outside space. I do not use the word garden here deliberately, since it does not accurately describe many of the locations where pots are particularly useful. They are one of the most practical ways of decorating roofs, decks, balconies, and windows, as well as the more usual ground-level areas.

**Contemporary or classic?**
Simple and modern, period and decorative – which is right for your small space?

## What can a pot do?

Pots not only make a strong statement of style through their shape, colour, and decoration, but when carefully positioned, they also help punctuate the layout of a small garden or even act as an eye-catching centrepiece. Containers are often the only feasible way of introducing planting into a confined or an awkward space.

The popular image of garden containers is of Mediterranean-style pots overflowing with colourful annuals. But there are many permutations in the relationship between pot and planting. Indeed, the right pot with no planting at all can assume a sculptural quality. In the 18th century, the boundaries between pot, plant, and sculpture were deliberately blurred by the use of lead plants in urns that were used as finials and the like. When choosing a container, ask yourself whether you want the pot, trough, or tub to be of main interest, rather than the plants you put in it? A lovely oil jar, for instance, can stand on its own without planting, providing visual pleasure in its shape. Or, at the other extreme, do you need a pot merely to hold compost, envisaging the plants as the main point of interest? Or perhaps you wish plant and pot to be of equal interest. Whatever the intended relationship of plant to pot is to be, it is important that the visual balance works.

**Regimented tulips** (above) Ranks of tulips are a good fit in slick, galvanized containers.

**Urban herbs** (left) Three silvered pots of lavender make a pleasing composition on a raised stand.

## Scale and style

Think also about how the shape and scale of your container will appear against its backdrop. Make sure that the style of your arrangement suits the mood of your garden. A jumble of pots can look very charming in the right environment – but beware, there is a very narrow dividing line between a jumble and a mess. A Classical-style urn, albeit made from reconstituted stone or fibreglass, is grand in style and may not be suited to a location that is humbler in feel. A pot that neither relates to the scale of a space nor the overall style can ruin the total effect.

**Pots within pots** (above) The grasses in these stainless steel planters themselves sit in composition pots, both to insulate the plants and for easy seasonal replacement.

**Charming jumble** (left) A delightful selection of plant material, suited to traditional terracotta. Be ruthless when a jumble becomes a mess.

## Materials

The natural materials from which containers are made include stone, reconstituted stone (stone that has been crushed, mixed with cement and/or resin, and then moulded), terracotta, wood, earthenware, and occasionally slate. Other materials that can look just as pleasing in the right place are concrete (possibly textured), metal, and a wide range of man-made synthetics, including fibreglass and plastic.

Containers that are to be kept outside all year round in cold climates should be made from a frost-resistant material, such as stone. Happily, most plants can be grown in most types of pot, as long as the compost is the appropriate kind and the drainage is adequate, so choose the pot that most suits the style of your garden and any envisaged planting. In a crisp, modern setting, you may well plump for the strong shapes of yuccas or cacti, best set off by a simply shaped container.

## Choosing a container

Though your choice may be tempered by economic considerations, many people are willing to spend a relatively large amount of money on garden containers. It may well be worth splashing out on a beautiful urn if it is to act as a permanent sculptural feature. However, why spend a lot on an imported Florentine pot only to conceal it with a mass of busy Lizzies, when a far cheaper, simple terracotta pot will do the same job?

If you want a container that you can move about the garden or take inside during the winter, bear in mind that its initial weight will be considerably increased by wet earth or compost. Incidentally, make sure that roofs and balconies are never overloaded with containers. Check with a structural engineer if you have any doubts. Where you have to be careful of overloading, use lightweight plant containers and position them at the side rather than in the middle of the roof, resting their weight on side walls when possible (but remember, this may be dangerous if there are strong winds).

## Positioning planted pots

As all plants are living, breathing things, they need care. Make sure that you locate planted containers where there is enough light and where you can reach plants to look after them. Those on a hot roof or exposed window-ledge will require water maybe twice a day, perhaps justifying an automatic irrigation system.

**Box row** This regimented line of clipped box in tall square metal containers creates visual interest in a small space to disguise the fencing panels behind.

## Focus on pots

Pots and containers are an ideal way of enlivening the smallest and most awkward of spaces, and can make a dramatic, witty, or subtle statement. A single container might act as an eye-catching centrepiece or a group of planted pots as your doorstep mini garden. Your choice of pot need by no means be limited to the purpose-made ones on the market, since plants can be grown in just about any receptacle (as long as you can make adequate drainage holes), which leaves plenty of scope for the inventive use of objects such as chimney pots or even old boots.

In the Mediterranean and Mexico, all sorts of cans, pots, and pans are colourfully planted and massed together, bringing colour and interest to windowsills, doorways, alleyways, and courtyards. Here is a selection of containers and planting of similar delight and ingenuity.

**Lilies in glass** (opposite top left) Whatever the container – here glass – I love lilies. They have a magnificent scale and deep fragrance.

**Traditional flower pots** (opposite top right) Hyacinths are wonderful for early spring scent, in this case presented in a ring of terracotta pots encircling grape hyacinths and *Lonicera fragrantissima*.

**Mixed media** (opposite bottom left) Good old pelargoniums will stand almost any treatment, even galvanized metal containers against sun-baked wooden boards.

**Box ball display** (opposite bottom right) White-painted pots unify this topiary collection.

"Think about how the shape and scale of your container will appear against its backdrop."

# Sculptural features

A small-space garden needs a feature to act as a visual "punctuation mark" in the layout or as the culmination of the overall design. Water can do it, seating can do it, and even people can do it, but when a garden has none of these, you will have to be more inventive.

If the design is modern, the feature might be sculpture; if traditional, statuary. For many, it is a kind of halfway house that is sought, since sculpture is often too expensive, and statuary too grand. It might instead be a pot or a collection of pots, a planted container, some boulders, a decorative wall plaque, a wall niche, or even the merest glimpse of a view, perhaps framed by a shuttered window frame that you insert in a wall. Whatever your choice, it should both catch the eye and give a raison d'être to the structure of the garden or its planting.

**Coiled serpent** (top) I can see children enjoying this serpent made of roof tiles.

**Crafted cockerel** (right) This handsome rooster might create just the right note within a small space—a touch of humor is a rare garden commodity!

**Delightful trickle** (opposite) These swaying disks, reminiscent of seashells, trickle with water and must look and sound delightful.

"A small-space garden needs a **feature** to act as a visual **punctuation mark**"

## Making a sculptural statement

Most of us tend to be very timid in our selection of external features, with the result that they do not make a strong enough statement within the garden's design, or are swamped by plants. Often this is because an object is placed too low, so that it is not visible when sitting down inside. Let its position be commanding, though not necessarily dominating, since half the secret of the correct siting of a feature outside is the way it is juxtaposed or counterbalanced with other objects—perhaps a tree, some seating, or even the view of a neighboring house. Traditionally, a feature, usually a statue, was placed right in the middle of the garden, but few outside spaces today have the kind of symmetry that calls for this type of classical positioning. Placing a feature to one side of an area is one way of lending movement to a layout, however small.

## Getting the scale right

Broadly speaking, the larger the object, the better it will do the job, since as well as providing a focal point within the garden, it should focus the view from inside the house, too. This is especially important when a space is too small or awkwardly placed to use, and serves just to be looked at through a door or from a window inside. Spotlit at night, an interesting sculptural feature outside will give your living space inside a whole new dimension and unify the entire inside/outside concept.

## Choosing a feature

It is all too easy to choose a feature that is too small, position it in the garden, and then, knowing that something is not quite right, add a pot nearby, followed by a specimen variegated shrub, in an effort to bolster its effect. The net result is that you draw attention to a disparate group of features and diminish the clarity of what you originally intended to be the eye-catcher. Choosing a feature that is in the correct scale for its setting is difficult, since you do have to choose the object in isolation from its intended setting, so try to carry in your mind's eye an optimum height and breadth. This will help you to get the scale right and ensure that your feature makes that vital visual punctuation mark.

**Thoughtful figure** (opposite, top left) "Quiet Contemplation," a piece in fiberglass by Marion Smith.

**Sinuous sculpture** (opposite, top right) Voluptuous white marble creates a dramatic focal point to this terrace.

**Faces in foliage** (opposite, bottom) A wonderful composition of heads and lotus leaves combines sculpture with planting.

**Sun on steel** (right) This dazzling piece in polished stainless steel glows in a beam of sunlight.

# Lighting

Outdoor lighting will maximize the pleasure you get from your small garden. It will enable you to eat, read, or simply potter around outside on warm spring and fall evenings, and, if you can see your garden from inside, enjoy a night-time view of it all year, giving the room you are in (inside or outside) an extra dimension of space. Outside lighting is essential in places where darkness falls early and the heat of the day makes escaping into the cool evening air a necessity. Even where summer evenings are long, some light, subtle artificial lighting will enhance the atmosphere of a meal outside or a party on a terrace and enable you to use your outside space to the fullest when dusk turns to darkness.

## Creative and functional lighting

Many people think of lighting a Christmas tree in the garden, but why stop there? Use lighting all through the year to create a gentle glow in the tracery of a fine specimen tree, to illuminate a group of pots, or to spotlight a piece of statuary, even in winter and under snow. Make the most of whatever features you have, especially if they are in a space you cannot actually use. If you live in the country, lighting will give you a hint of the wildness beyond your own small patch. Other kinds of lighting have primarily a functional rather than a decorative purpose—such as that between the garage and the front door or alongside a flight of steps, or brilliant security lighting.

**Sympathetic combination** (opposite) Permanent uplighters highlight strong foliage shapes, while incidental lanterns add to the ambiance.

**Spiral attraction** (above) Ground-level uplighters are a key feature of this spiraling wall piece, attracting us to the central seating area.

## Creating the effect you want

Decide on exactly what you want lit and the kind of effect you are after. Be practical—appealing as subtle half-lighting might be, if you are cooking on the grill or pouring a drink, you will end up in a mess. For this sort of activity and for lighting paths and steps, you need a direct source of light. Position the light fixture near the area you want lit, but low enough to avoid creating an eerie effect; bulkhead fittings set into walls do the trick perfectly. For eating outside or reading, you can use a simple outdoor table lamp. Install outlets with ground fault interrupters in different places so that you can move the light around. For special occasions, there is nothing more pleasing than the gentle flicker of candlelight; this, combined with indoor lighting, may be all you need to illuminate a small space near the home.

**After a downpour** (above) Lighting and wet surfaces create a striking effect in this minimal space, dramatizing stems, foliage, and a water feature.

**Overall glow** (opposite left) Locating several gentle light sources correctly will achieve a pleasing overall level of illumination in the garden.

**Attractive posts** (center, top) These stainless steel posts incorporate lighting to define an entrance path. They will look just as good during the day.

**Tread carefully** (center, bottom) It is very important to illuminate step treads on regular routes. Center the lights, as here, or position them to the side.

**Mini uplighters** (right, top) Networks of mini uplighters are a relatively new option. Their combined illumination can create an attractive effect across a terrace or along a pathway.

**Among plantings** (right, bottom) Nestling within plantings, uplighters will cast dramatic shadows.

## Light fixtures and installation

Choose light fixtures that are practical and suit the style of your outside room; if in doubt, choose a simple, strong, and unobtrusive design. It is vital that you use light fixtures specially designed for outside use and that they are professionally wired and installed. All light fixtures, wires, and outlets must be waterproof and armored where they might be damaged by a rake or shovel when in the process of gardening.

# Fabrics

In a large space, the impact of chair covers, cushions, umbrellas, and awnings is diluted by the amount of vegetation and space that lies between them. In a small garden space, however, fabrics really come into their own, giving a sense of softness and luxury that makes up for the lack of vegetation, and creating a comfortable and inviting roomlike environment.

**Complementary** (above) The fabric of a tablecloth and upholstery cushions softens this magical afternoon setting.

**Kite in the jungle** (opposite) A high-tech triangle of fabric creates a tented shade among lush surroundings .

## Structures and furnishings

A fabric "ceiling," in the form of an awning, will either shade you from the sun or enable you to be outside, oblivious to the gray skies overhead. If you are overlooked from above, it will also afford you privacy. Small standard-shaped awnings, designed either to be attached to a wall at one end or to be supported by a frame and thus freestanding, can be bought in kit form. If your space is awkwardly shaped, you may need to design or make your own. A swag awning can be made by attaching fabric to the underside of an arbor's horizontals. Large sunshades make ideal portable, temporary "ceilings" for small gardens. They can be positioned in just the right place over a table or lounger and are easily folded up and stored away. Vertical "walls" of fabric will give you privacy from neighbors' yards and shelter from chilling winds.

Chair covers, cushions, rugs, and tablecloths are all possible seasonal additions to your outside space and can have more impact than plants. Taken outside on a sunny day and grouped around a rug, large cushions will transform your balcony, roof-top, or ground-level garden into an inviting and comfortable room in which to relax.

**Provençal feel** (below) All the comforts of the inside, but out. The styling is Provençal, complete with overhead dappling shade.

**Instant venue** (below right) A simple white parasol is hard to beat—open it up and there is a conversation venue in its welcoming shade.

## Choosing fabrics

Fabrics for outside use should be tough, preferably washable, and suit the style of your garden space. Patterned fabrics hide the dirt better than plain ones and so are particularly useful in dusty cities.

Take fabric samples outside and visualize what they will look like there, in the form of a chair cover or umbrella, in relation to the color of your garden's structures and other "furnishings." A hard-working fabric, such as canvas or sailcloth, should be used for the weather side of awnings; the underside can be lined, or softly swagged with a more delicate fabric for an exotic tented effect—think of the colorful awnings with braiding and mirrored inlays depicted in Indian and Persian paintings.

**Year-round awning** (above left) A simple awning such as this can remain in place all summer. Its scale works well with the wall beyond.

**Splash of yellow** (above right) The yellow of these upholstered director's chairs sings out even in the shade of a large parasol.

**Sculptural additions** (opposite) Well-built and weatherproofed traditional Adirondack chairs are both sculptural and durable enough to stay out all season. They are comfortable, too.

**Upholstered set** (right) All the seating shown here—light metal furniture for a balcony, a sharp-lined lounger in the shade, and a traditional garden bench—are enlivened by their upholstery.

# Freestanding furniture

Whatever the size of your garden, its furniture should be an integral part of your whole design, rather than an afterthought. But when space is limited, it is especially important to think about furniture from the planning stage onward. So ask yourself plenty of questions. Do you ever work or write outside? Do you need furniture that can withstand being used by children as an adventure playground? Or would you like a bench where you can briefly pause in the shade, or a table near the kitchen door so that you can prepare food in the fresh air?

"it is especially important to think about **furniture** from the **planning** stage onward."

## Relating shapes and colors

The way in which the shape and bulk of a grouping of furniture, or a single bench, relates to the rest of the garden is as important as how you plan the massing of plant material. Both are part of the balance of the garden. Consider not only the practical aspects of your furniture, but also how its style suits that of your garden and house, and the impact of its shape and color. It is important to decide whether your furniture will be in the garden year-round, in which case it will in effect be a permanent part of the garden's structure, or if its presence will be temporary, maybe there for just a few months or days. Furniture that is a permanent fixture should have a settled look, and a bulk and stability in scale with its surroundings. Often, the most satisfactory way of achieving this is by having built-in furniture. An eye-catching piece of garden furniture can become a sculptural feature in its own right and perhaps inspire your choice of materials and other aspects of your garden's design.

Furniture that is outside for limited periods should not give the appearance of ill-considered clutter. Make sure, too, that an area such as a terrace where furniture is temporarily arranged for entertaining does not look neglected and unwelcoming when cleared. Try to visualize what your garden space will look like without as well as with furniture.

Comfort and practicality on one hand and stylish design on the other need not be mutually exclusive, though to look at much garden furniture on the market, this might seem so. It is worth hunting around for pieces that are functional as well as aesthetically pleasing. Violently colored, hectically patterned upholstery may look fine in brilliant sunshine or against an azure sea, but out of place and gaudy in a gray-skied suburban garden. Always consider how the color of your furniture is affected by the quality of natural light in your garden. I have been experimenting with tones of blue in my own garden for years.

## Choosing a style

So what is the ideal? Furniture constructed from natural materials and upholstered in neutral colors tends to fit more comfortably with natural forms, as do curving organic shapes. However, the "natural" may not necessarily be in keeping with the location of your outside space, the architecture of your house, or the style of its interior decor and furnishing. Every material has its own character, and it may be that the hard look of a sleek metal chair suits the feel of your urban balcony and echoes the chic style of the room from which it leads.

## Furniture as a visual link

If a beautifully designed and constructed chair is the key to linking interior and exterior, it is worth the investment. In a limited space, the visual connection between the two is particularly important. The division between them can either be softened by having furniture that is akin in style to that inside, or by linking the two in the color or texture of upholstery. When arranging furniture outside, it is important to consider what it will look like from inside, too.

**More than a seat** (above left) This piece is both sculpture and seating. Its wonderful shape of connected ellipses could help determine the layout for a whole garden.

**Seasonal set piece** (left) A traditional set of wickerwork furniture in the shade of a tree.

**Back-friendly** (opposite) This roll-edged style of park bench is a terrific relaxant for people with back problems. It is handsome, too.

## Ensuring comfort

Choose furniture that suits its function as well as being good to look at. A chair used for sitting at a table for meals should not only provide back support and be at a suitable height and angle to the table, but should be comfortable enough to linger in, since long, lazy summer lunches and dinners on the deck can be memorable occasions. Ornate iron and lookalike aluminum seating seldom provides this comfort, unlike canvas-seated director's chairs or simple pine kitchen furniture.

For reading the Sunday paper or a book outside, bucket-shaped chairs are perfect; even glider loveseats (though to my mind hideous contraptions) are undeniably comfortable. Lightweight, folding chairs, though easily stored and ideal for impromptu seating, are completely unsuited to true sybaritic pleasure. Sunbathing beds, such as those found on French and Italian beaches, are practical, comfortable, and attractive, unlike those with wheels and handles and collapsible backrests, which require lots of storage space and feats of patient endurance to click into position. The lines of a small swimming pool are far better enhanced by simple furniture than that which is "fussy" and cumbersome. Try to find garden furniture that fits in with your lifestyle. To my mind, much that is available may not do so, swinging as it does between self-conscious elegance on the one hand and rustic "old-fashioned" charm on the other.

**Summer pleasure** (top) All ready for a weekend in the sun, but where will you store them in winter? A lightly patterned fabric would avoid perspiration marks.

**Portable comfort** A picnic table and chairs that could travel with you, and yet are robust enough to be comfortable.

## Materials

Well-seasoned wood will last a lifetime and withstand hot sun, rain, and frost. It is also the easiest material to use for making your own furniture. Left natural and finished with a clear preservative, it blends in well with the natural forms of a garden. Painted, it can add a new dimension, and bring out the color of a neighboring wall or door.

Metal takes kindly to modern design, though not to humidity. Unless it is plastic-coated, it will require regular repainting to prevent it from becoming rusty and looking neglected. Plastic, on the other hand, requires no maintenance, and is practical for all climates and light enough to be portable, but, unlike a material such as stone, it does not weather pleasingly with age.

**Fold-away** Lightweight folding chairs are perhaps the best option for small gardens, as long as you have somewhere to store them in winter.

**Bench feature** (top) An incidental bench can be used to stand pots on or for taking a break.

**Dining support** (above) Sturdy dining chairs made for long weekend lunches in summer.

"an effective way of making the **most** of the space"

**Sculptural presence versus comfort** (below) For restricted space, the built-in bench and table takes up less room, but it has to be comfortable, too—and look good with pots in winter.

**Generous dimensions** (opposite) Ensure that dimensions are generous when building your furniture. This is ideal for laying a tray on, for lying on with a mattress, and for dining.

# Built-in furniture

Building furniture into the structure of your garden is an effective way of making the most of the space you have, both visually and physically. The most important advantage, visually, is that furniture that is treated as an integral part of the overall design (constructed from a material that blends in well with surrounding structures) gives a small area a unified look, making it appear larger. Built-in furniture also helps avoid the clutter often created by freestanding chairs and tables, and solves the problem of where to store them. Even the smallest freestanding table with a chair on either side needs a minimum 6 ft (2 m) of clear space, and this is a considerable amount in a very cramped site.

## Using existing features

Existing features can be modified to make seating space, or new features designed so that they have a dual function. Raising the wall around an existing pool, for instance, will provide you with an area on which to sit or stand pots. Retaining walls around a bed can be designed so that they are at a suitable height for casual seating. Raised brick or concrete slabs ("pads"), designed as a permanent part of a garden's pattern, can be used as a low table or for seating; when not in use, they will blend in naturally with the rest of the garden. Existing trees, which often occupy rather high proportions of space in a small garden, can be used to save space at ground level by being employed as a support for a hammock, for example, or light fixtures. Large trees can be put to good use for children; they can become home to a treehouse or used to support a swing, rope ladder, or knotted length of rope. Play features like this can easily be dismantled when the children grow older. When building a play area with a more permanent structure, it is wise to have an alternative use in mind for later years. A raised sandbox, for example, could be later used as a water feature and its walls as casual seating.

## Materials

To create a unified look, choose materials that complement the rest of the garden. If using wood, choose a hardwood, since softwoods tend to splinter. Concrete is cheap and durable, but austere. Its appearance can be softened, however, by hanging plants, for example, or by combining it with another material, such as wood. Brick is one of the most useful materials, since its small unit size makes it possible to build furniture in awkward spaces.

**Harmony** (opposite, top) Use of the same hardwood for the floor as well as the table and benches, together with a stylish reinterpretation of the bamboo screen, creates a really harmonious roof-garden setting.

**Seat plus storage** (opposite, bottom left) A bench seat in a cupboard recess. The more storage you have out there, the better.

**Simply perfect** (opposite bottom right) Nothing could be more simple and effective than this built-in bench. Notice the discreet light built into the wall beneath the bench.

**Tree seat** (below) A circular bench seat to focus the eye on a special tree is an age-old idea worth revisiting.

# planting

The sheer number of plants available can make selecting those that suit both the location and style of your small space seem a daunting prospect.

**Opposite** A mix of woody shrubs, perennials, and bulbs creates a colorful display in this small garden.

# Garden "software"

Though I agree with Thomas Church's philosophy that "gardens are for people," plants are important, too, since they help your outside room to become your breathing space—a place to escape from the pressures of everyday life. The sights, sounds, and smells of plants are a great restorative, and for many people, tending them is wonderfully relaxing.

Plants that are used to enhance the style and mood of your outside space should be treated as an integral part of its design—the shape of your bed or arrangement of planted containers, for instance, should relate to the scale of a paved area, and the colors of your plants to surrounding colors. It is a myth that small spaces need peppering with small details and ornate, miniaturized planting schemes—quite the reverse. Bold, simple planting schemes, created from a limited range of plant material, are nearly always the most effective.

Planting design is about manipulating multiple quantities of plant material. Do not attempt to dive in at the deep end and try to create a border worthy of Gertrude Jekyll at the first attempt. One of the joys of planting is seeing the right balance develop and moving plants around each fall as you seek to create the wonderful image you hold in your mind's eye.

**Seasonal show** (opposite) An autumnal mood is created with yellow flowering perennials, including heleniums and various types of rudbeckia.

**Evergreen stars** (above right) Sedum heads are fleshy and strongly architectural. This example is *Sedum rosea*, whose stems are eventually topped by lime-green, starry flowers.

"Plants help your outside room to become your breathing space"

# Planning your planting

Many gardeners, small-space or otherwise, are content for their garden to be a collection of their favorite plants, "arranged" in a sequence. But your carefully planned structure deserves plants that suit its scale and that will act as the catalyst to bring your garden to life.

### Choosing plants

To begin with, only use plants you are familiar with—look them up in a catalog or directory, and check the "feel" of them at a plant nursery or garden center. This may well limit you to a small range of material, but this is all to the good, since too much variety of plant form and shape can lead to a staccato, "party mix" effect, instead of the harmonious blend of plant forms and colors you should be seeking to create. The next step is to classify your plant material, working down in scale from the largest to the smallest.

### 1 Feature plants

First, decide what your key plants or "specials" are going to be. These can be used as a visual link between your planting and the surrounding architecture—for instance, a weeping cherry curving over a pool wall. On a smaller scale, the "special" might be a yucca acting as an evergreen pivot within a group of perennials. You could even have a major and a minor "special," counterbalancing one another within the overall design.

### 2 Skeleton plants

Next, choose your skeleton planting. This should be evergreen so that it provides a permanent structure and background to the rest of your plants and its bulk reinforces the design of your garden, screening and providing shelter where necessary. Plan ahead when planting, particularly in the case of evergreen shrubs, many of which take a long time to mature. Try to envision how the plants will look in five years, and space them accordingly. Make a plan of your garden and shade in the evergreens to get a clear idea of the space left. You can use quick fillers to plug the gaps while the skeleton planting matures.

### Decorative fill

3 Having selected your skeleton plants, you can start to think about the style or mood you want your planting scheme to have and to choose seasonally decorative shrubs (again, working down in scale from large to small). Group shrubs so that they are in scale with the design of your garden; the width of the terrace they border, for instance, or the height of a fence or tree behind them. Avoid using too many single decorative filler plants; they might detract from the effectiveness of the "specials."

### The "pretties"

4 The next step is to choose what I call "pretties." Into this category come smaller shrubby species, such as *Santolina* spp., some *Hebe* spp., all the perennials, and many herbs. Unless working on the tiniest scale, these should be planted in masses as well, with an eye to the way the texture and color of their foliage in particular (this outlasts flower color) relates to the plants around them. Finally, consider fillers— bulbs, such as tulips and irises, self-seeding biennials, annuals, such as sunflowers, and ground-cover plants, such as hostas and ajuga, all come into this category.

# Making a planting plan

Your planting scheme should be conceived in relation to your overall design and used to soften and overlay its hard structures. The best way to plan your planting is to indicate the position and approximate spread of fully mature plants on a scaled plan. The planting plan shown here follows the way you evolve your sequence as described on the previous two pages.

**1 Feature plants**
The "special"—in this case, a fruiting tree.

**2 Skeleton plants**
The skeletal filler material features a euphorbia in the foreground, with a *Phormium tenax* beyond.

**3 Decorative fill**
A variety of decorative shrubs have been planted behind the tree.

**4 The "pretties"**
These mostly consist of chrysanthemums, with a tall aconitum beside the tree and on the right.

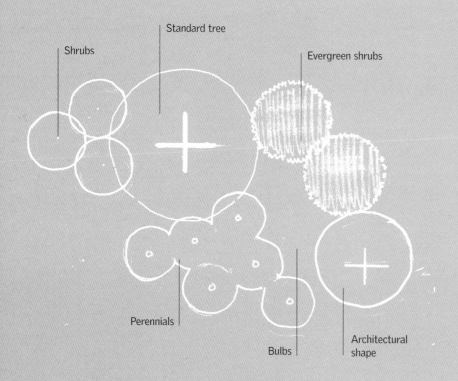

Shrubs

Standard tree

Evergreen shrubs

Perennials

Bulbs

Architectural shape

# Plants for color

Color is a rejuvenator and revives the spirits, and many city-dwellers use brightly colored planting as a relief from the monotonous grays and browns around them. When choosing plants, consider not only the temporary flamboyance of annual flower color, but the more permanent displays of foliage, stem, branch, and bark. Foliage colors range from all the many shades of green, through to gold, bronze, purple, and silver, while stem and branch colors include yellows, greens, browns, and reds. These should be combined to create year-round displays that will provide a foil for seasonal flower color.

## Linking color

Whether your garden consists of a few pots on a balcony or a few planters in a basement entrance, try to tailor your range of plants so that their color blends well with the surroundings. You have to remember that every element in a limited space, from walls and paving to chair-cover fabric, will be seen in unison. Peppering a small space with many contrasted colors that have no link to one another or their surroundings will create a random, disparate appearance; creating a harmonious composition by linking colors will unify your space and make it appear larger.

## The impact of color

The impact of the color of each plant in a scheme will vary according to its size, so when planning a scheme, bear in mind the dimensions to which each plant will grow and how this will affect the distribution of different colors. Try to visualize the effect of shade or sunshine on different colors, since this can radically alter their qualities. Red, for instance, is a demanding color that is hard to use outside, especially in bright sun, but in a shaded area, it can be effectively combined with grays, purples, and pinks.

**Color enhancer** (above left) The hue of the appropriately named Japanese blood grass, *Imperata cylindrica* 'Rubra', is emphasized by its container.

**One-color scheme** (left) A single, strong red, with just a touch of deep purple, punctuates this mass of architectural foliage forms.

**Color and form** (opposite) Vertical lavender flower forms are contrasted with pink spherical allium heads in a late spring arrangement.

# Silver and gray

There are many plants with gray and silver foliage, and they can be combined to create a scheme with a light, airy atmosphere. The intensity of their color varies according to the texture and density of their foliage, and they can be arranged so that some parts of a scheme have an ethereal quality and others a bold appearance. Gray and silver plants usually prefer a hot, sunny position and dry soil.

### 1 *Helichrysum italicum*
**Curry Plant**

Commonly known as the curry plant, this neat bush has a strongly aromatic scent to its foliage. It has clusters of small, yellow flowers and grows to about 2 ft (60 cm) high.

### 2 *Salvia argentea*
**Sage**

This is very much a feature plant, with crinkly gray leaves whitened by a silky down. It bears stems of white hooded flowers and grows to about 2 ft (60 cm) high.

### 3 *Lamium maculatum* 'Beacon Silver'
**Dead Nettle**

This is a useful ground-cover plant in a partly shaded, cool garden, which can be grown under taller shrubs. It grows to 4 in (10 cm) high.

### 4 *Artemisia* 'Powis Castle'
**Wormwood**

This species is similar to *A. arborescens*, and both are firm favorites, with a soft gray, filigree foliage. It likes hot and dry conditions and grows 2–3 ft (60–90 cm) high.

### 5 *Stachys byzantina* 'Silver Carpet'
**Lamb's-Ears, Lamb's-Tongue**

This is a nonflowering lamb's-ear or lamb's-tongue, which forms a silver mass that is useful for edging a bed or as a not-too-dense ground cover. It grows to 5 in (12 cm) high.

6

7

8

9

### 6 *Hedera helix* 'Glacier'
**Common Ivy**

This self-clinging evergreen has small, silver-gray leaves with a white edging. It is suitable for any exposure and is frost-hardy. It has a height and spread of 10 x 10 ft (3 x 3 m).

### 7 *Cynara cardunculus*
**Cardoon**

A great architectural plant for early in the year, this decorative cousin of the artichoke dies back in midsummer. It has huge, handsome gray leaves and is only suitable for the largest of small gardens. It grows to 6 ft (2 m) high.

### 8 *Verbascum bombyciferum*
**Mullein**

A biennial, the giant mullein has rosettes of long, oval, gray-white leaves, from which rise 6-ft (2-m) spikes that carry yellow flowers.

### 9 *Santolina pinnata* ssp. *neopolitana*
**Santolina**

This dwarf shrub bears small, button, yellow flowers on feathery, gray foliage. It forms a neat bush up to about 2 ft (60 cm) high.

### 10 *Senecio Cineraria* 'Silver Dust'
**Senecio**

This senecio has lobed silver-gray leaves with their undersides and stems coated with white down. It can be killed by frost or, in warmer climates, by winter rain. It grows to about 20 in (50 cm) high.

### 11 *Ruta graveolens* 'Jackman's Blue'
**Rue**

Rue has blue-gray foliage and a strongly aromatic fragrance when the leaves are pinched. It is a good edging plant and grows to about 1½ ft (45 cm) high.

# Purple

Purple is a demanding color (more common in foliage than in flower), and difficult to incorporate within a mixed group. However, an arrangement of varying shades of purple has a spectacular effect and creates a moody atmosphere. Of the few evergreen, purple-foliaged shrubs, most belong to the barberry family.

### 1 Weigela florida 'Foliis Purpureis'
**Weigela**

A shrub that flowers in June, with rose-pink blooms that contrast well with the foliage. It prefers rich, moist soil and reaches a height and spread of 4 x 4 ft (1.2 x 1.2 m).

### 2 Erysimum 'Bowles Mauve'
**Wallflower**

This is a remarkable wallflower, continuing its dark and light purple flowering for weeks, although the flowers have no scent. It grows to 3 ft (90 cm) high.

### 3 Saxifraga oppositifolia var. latina
**Saxifraga**

This saxifraga's low cushion of green foliage looks good all year, and is especially effective when grown to spill out of a raised bed. The late spring flowers are a bonus. It has a height and spread of 2 x 8 in (5 x 20 cm).

### 4 Berberis gagnepainii 'Wallchiana Purpurea'
**Barberry**

A prickly shrub that thrives in dry soil and in most situations. This form is evergreen with erect-growing branches, yellow leaves, and narrow, crinkly leaves. It grows 2¾–4 ft (80 cm–1.2 m) in height.

### 5 Sedum telephium 'Atropurpureum'
**Stonecrop**

This sedum makes a dramatic feature plant. In late summer, its flower heads combine rosy pink and brown, eventually forming chocolate-brown seed heads. It grows to a height of 1½ ft (45 cm).

### 6 *Ajuga reptans* 'Atropurpurea'
**Common Bugle**

A ground-covering plant for a moist situation, this bugle has a good contrast of deep blue flowers with burnished-purple foliage. It grows to 8 in (20 cm) high.

### 7 *Salvia officinalis* Purpurascens Group
**Purple Sage**

I love this woody plant, although it needs to be replaced every three years or so. The young foliage is soft gray-purple contrasting with purple-blue flowers. It grows to 2 ft (60 cm) high.

# 8

## *Cotinus coggyria*
## Smoke Bush, Smoke Tree

There are various forms of this smoke bush or smoke tree, offering varying degrees of purple in their foliage. It prefers a light soil and can be rampant, with a height and spread of 6 x 5 ft (1.8 x 1.5 m).

# 9

## *Hebe* 'Mrs. Winder'
## Shrubby Veronica

All veronicas are evergreen and well suited to most situations except the coldest and wettest. Not all are frost-hardy. 'Mrs. Winder' has purplish-bronze foliage and bright-blue flowers. It grows to 2 ft (60 cm) high.

# Gold and yellow

Gold is a warm and sunny color that will brighten any area, even on a dull day. Gold foliage combines well with green, cream, lemon, and yellow flower colors—blue could be added for a touch of excitement.

1 *Hypericum calycinum*
**Rose of Sharon**

Hypericums are really tough shrubs. This form is evergreen and will thrive in any soil. It prefers shade or half shade. It grows up to 12 in (30 cm) high and its spread is indefinite.

2 *Helichrysum splendidum*
**Helichrysum**

This compact, evergreen bush has silvery-gray, felty leaves, with clusters of tiny yellow flowers in midsummer. This is a plant for a hot, dry garden, growing up to 4 ft (1.2 m) high.

### 3 *Oenothera missouriensis*
### Evening Primrose

This is a lovely evening/nighttime plant for somewhere hot and dry. Lemon yellow flowers, which remain closed for most of the day but open in the late afternoon, smother the delicate foliage. It is a great self-seeder. It grows to a height of 9 in (23 cm).

### 4 *Primula bulleyana*
### Primula

This candelabra-type yellow primula blooms in May and June. It can be grown in either sun or shade but must be kept moist. Its height is about 1½ ft (45 cm).

### 5 *Ilex aquifolium* 'Golden Milkboy'
### Variegated Holly

Although slow-growing, holly is a splendid evergreen. It grows in any well-drained soil in half- or full shade. It does not like extreme wetness or drought.

### 6 *Lysimachia nummularia* 'Aurea'
### Golden Creeping Jenny

As its common name suggests, this little plant—only 2 in (5 cm) high—is a ground cover with bright-gold foliage. It prefers a cool soil and a dampish situation.

### 7 *Sambucus racemosa* 'Plumosa Aurea'
### Golden Cut-Leaved Elder

Elders are excellent quick-growing shrubs in almost any situation, and as tough as old boots. Although not evergreen, they offer many interesting leaf forms.

8 *Melissa officinalis* 'Aurea'
**Lemon Balm, Bee Balm**

The foliage of this lemon-scented perennial has distinctive, rich-yellow patterning all season. Growing it in partial shade will prevent leaf scorch. It grows to 2 ft (60 cm) high.

9 *Euonymus fortunei* 'Emerald 'n' Gold'
**Spindle Tree**

This hummock-forming evergreen shrub turns bronzy pink in the fall. Tolerant of most situations, it is excellent for borders or tubs for year-round interest. It has a height and spread of 18 x 24 in (45 x 60 cm).

# Red and orange

Not to everyone's taste, these demanding colors brighten up a dark corner and suit a high-activity location. Used in conjunction with gold-foliaged plants, or ones with gray or purple leaves, wonderful effects can be achieved in an artificial situation, such as a roof-space or in an urban garden. Growing naturally in a general planting, these are the quintessential colors of fall in a temperate climate.

### 1 *Hibiscus rosa-sinensis* 'Scarlet Giant'
**Rose of China**

For a flamboyant or tropical effect from midsummer onward, this is your plant. It will grow in any well-drained soil, although sun is essential. Its height and spread are 6 x 6 ft (1.8 x 1.8 m).

### 2 *Dahlia* 'Grenadier'
**Dahlia**

I am increasingly fond of dahlias, and in warmer areas, their corms can be left in the ground through the winter, as long as the soil is well drained. Many different types, with varying flower head forms, are available, this variety being classified as "decorative," and some have attractive bronze- or purple-hued foliage. The larger-headed forms often need staking. Its height and spread are 24 in (60 x 60 cm).

### 3 *Hemerocallis* 'Stafford'
**Day lily**

Day lilies are always useful if all else fails, but recent hybridizing has thrown up some really lovely flowering forms, such as this example. Their foliage is some of the earliest to appear in spring. Later, these grassy clumps provide useful ground cover. Flowers are an added bonus. They can be grown in any soil, except the very dry, and in sun or shade. The height of this variety is 28 in (70 cm).

### 4 *Hemerocallis fulva*
**Day lily**

An alternative variety of day lily with variegated leaves, its orange flowers have distinctive coppery-red patterns. Its height can be up to 4 ft (1.2 m).

## 5 *Scabiosa atropurpurea* 'Ace of Spades'
### Sweet Scabious

Scabious are useful perennials for the small garden, growing to about 2½ ft (75 cm), and looking lovely mixed with other perennials or grasses. *S. atropurpurea* has wonderfully deep crimson flower heads, produced from midsummer through to early fall.

## 6 *Cosmos atrosanguineus*
### Chocolate Cosmos

As an annual filler, cosmos is hard to beat. It flowers all through the summer and into fall, and is available in white, pink, red, and this lovely black-red color. As an added bonus, these flowers have a chocolaty fragrance. Plant en masse for impact. This species grows to a height of about 2½ ft (75 cm).

7

8

## 7 *Rosa rugosa* 'Roseraie de l'Haÿ'
### Shrub Rose

Rugosa roses are perpetual-flowering, bushy shrub roses, with good disease-resistant foliage and well-scented blooms. A hybrid rugosa, this form has purple-crimson flowers, with long and shapely buds—a real winner. It is vigorous and tough even in poor soils. It has a height and spread of 6 x 6 ft (1.8 x 1.8 m).

## 8 *Hydrangea macrophylla* 'Hamburg'
### Hydrangea

This well-known hydrangea has pink flower heads, though in acidic soil they will be blue. In fall, the heads assume a deep red. It prefers rich, well-drained soil. Leave the flower heads in place through the winter, to give protection to young buds, then remove in March. Prune out weak growth and old wood after flowering.

# Blue

As a color in the garden, I find blue very seldom out of place—it can be soft and calming or robust and vigorous. It is wonderfully effective when used in conjunction with a "lap" or plunge pool, yet it is equally at home in a perennial or meadow planting.

### 3 *Hydrangea serrata* 'Bluebird'
### Hydrangea

This hydrangea has lacecap-type flower heads. The heads are flat, with small, mid-blue, central (fertile) flowers and an outer ring of pale pink "ray florets" (or blue if growing in acidic soil)—the larger, sterile flowers. It has an eventual height and spread of 4 x 4 ft (1.2 x 1.2 m).

### 4 *Buddleja davidii* 'Empire Blue'
### Butterfly Bush

A fast-growing shrub that is invaluable for creating a quick effect. It has long, tapering leaves and scented flowers of rich violet blue with an orange eye that are very attractive to butterflies during July and August. It can be grown in any soil and is best in full sun. It has a height and spread of 8¼ x 6 ft (2.5 x 1.8 m), but its size can be limited by pruning.

### 1 *Echinops ritro*
### Globe Thistle

It is not only the color but the shape of this plant that makes it statuesque, even in the poorest soil. Tall gray stems rise out of silvery, spiky foliage, bearing steel blue flowers in late summer. This relatively compact form grows to a height of about 2½ ft (75 cm).

### 2 *Iris sibirica* 'Perry's Blue'
### Siberian Flag

This graceful iris, with its foliage, will grow either by the waterside or in any good, ordinary soil as long as it remains moist. It grows to about 2½ ft (75 cm) high.

**5**

**6**

### 5 *Eryngium bourgatii* 'Oxford Blue'
**Eryngo**

This is a spectacular foliage plant, with deeply divided, prickly edged, silver-veined leaves. The distinctive flower heads of blue-green are conspicuous all summer. It reaches a height of 2 ft (60 cm).

### 6 *Festuca glauca* 'Blue Fox'
**Festuca**

This grass is hard and spiky, with steel-blue stems, and offers an interesting contrast in texture to fleshy shrubs and perennials. It requires the driest of soils and full sun. It has a height and spread of about 8 x 9 in (20 x 23 cm).

## 7 *Agapanthus campanulatus* 'Blue Giant'
### Blue African Lily

This agapanthus is hardy in mild climates if grown in well-drained soil. A winter mulch is advisable, however, if in a relatively exposed site. The plant's extravagant flower heads, which appear in August, epitomize high summer. It is perfect for pots or tubs. It grows to about 3 ft (90 cm) high.

## 8 *Penstemon* 'Sour Grapes'
### Penstemon

I have become increasingly fond of penstemons for their impressive flowering performance. The color of this cultivar is like that of unripe grapes—soft amethyst and blue. It will flower in any well-drained soil from July to October, and reaches a height of around 2 ft (60 cm).

# Lemon and white

I love white flowers, which look especially effective among a mass of green foliage. White and gray is a subtle, sophisticated color combination. Too much color can become tiring in a garden, but white is always refreshing, both during the day and at night—something that cannot be said for many colors.

### 1 *Romneya coulteri* var. *trichocalyx* 'White Cloud'
**California Tree Poppy**

The California tree poppy has one of the purest white flowers, with bright yellow stamens, and this form has attractive gray foliage. Its origins dictate its requirements—well-drained soil and a south-facing site. It is slow to establish, but subsequently produces persistent underground suckers. It is therefore not suitable for growing in a container. It can grow to a height of 5 ft (1.5 m).

### 2 *Narcissus poeticus* var. *recurvus*
**Pheasant's-Eye Narcissus**

There are many forms of white narcissus, but this one has strongly scented flowers with a small central, red-rimmed cup—hence the name "pheasant's-eye." The bulb flowers late in the spring and grows to about 14 in (36 cm) high.

### 3 *Leucanthemella serotina*
**Leucanthemella**

This is a useful perennial to grow through shrubs for late flowering in October. Strong clumps of 7½-ft- (2.3-m-) high, stiff stems are topped by sprays of green-eyed, chalk-white, daisy flowers that are excellent for cutting.

3

5

6

## 5 *Primula vulgaris*
### Primrose

Nothing heralds spring more positively than the sight of banks of the common primrose. I love its pale yellow color. It prefers light shade and damp soil.

## 6 *Crambe cordifolia*
### Crambe

Spectacular flowers reminiscent of gypsophila rise during July from coarse green leaves, which soon die off. Therefore, it is best to mix this 6-ft 92-m) beauty through fall-flowering shrubs, where the plant will disappear until the following year.

### 7 *Kniphofia* 'Little Maid'
**Red-Hot Poker**

This variety has green flower spikes when in bud, which then open to white and last for weeks through the fall. The foliage is neat and narrow and the plant is smaller in size than other red-hot pokers, reaching about 2 ft (60 cm).

### 8 *Helleborus hybridus* 'Citron'
**Hellebore**

I don't think we value hellebores enough, since they are not only sculpturally evergreen but also have these beautiful cup-shaped flowers that are so welcome in early spring. They will grow anywhere with good drainage, but they do require a soil enriched with organic matter.

# Climbers

Climbers are invaluable in the small-space garden. Not only do they make it possible to enjoy plants for their own sake, without using up valuable ground space, but they can be used to soften hard structures visually or disguise ugly ones and, in conjunction with an arbor or openwork fencing, provide privacy, shade, and shelter.

### Types of climbers

Some climbers, such as ivy (*Hedera* spp.), have suckerlike roots that attach themselves to vertical surfaces and require no additional form of support. Others, such as sweet peas (*Lathyrus odoratus*) and *Clematis* spp., have small tendrils that twist and twine around a support such as a trellis, openwork fencing, or a host plant. In addition to these true climbers, there are plants, such as *Cotoneaster horizontalis*, that will push themselves up a vertical surface. These can be contrasted with those that hang downward, such as *Cotoneaster dammeri*. Many shrubs that are perfectly at home in the open, such as *Magnolia grandiflora*, will, if supported and pruned into shape, happily grow tall and upright when planted against a vertical surface.

### Supporting climbers

Trellises and wires can be used to support climbers; wires provide the most imperceptible support, but are not suitable for heavy climbers. A trellis can be used purely as a plant support, in which case it should dominate neither the wall nor the plant, or as a decorative feature in its own right, the plant acting merely as a cosmetic softener, in which case it should be eye-catching, perhaps painted a bright color or large in relation to the scale of the plant.

### 1 *Hedera helix* 'Goldheart'
### English Ivy

This self-climbing, hardy evergreen climber is suitable for any exposure. It has elegant green leaves with a golden-yellow center. It is slow-growing until it can attach itself to a support. It grows up to 4 ft (1.2 m) tall.

### 2 *Parthenocissus tricuspidata*
### Boston Ivy

This very vigorous, deciduous climber has vinelike leaves that give a dazzling fall display of red and crimson. It will grow in any exposure, but be sure to keep it out of gutters. It has a height and spread of 23 x 20 ft (7 x 6 m).

### 3 *Solanum crispum* 'Glasnevin'
### Chilean Potato Tree

This is a wall plant for a sheltered site with a southern or western exposure, but for any soil. It bears clusters of rich purple-blue flowers from July to October. It has a height and spread of 13 x 3 ft (4 x 1 m).

6

7

8

### 6 *Lonicera brownii* 'Dropmore Scarlet'
**Scarlet Trumpet Honeysuckle**

This particular honeysuckle has no scent to its bright-scarlet, tubular flowers, which appear from July to October. It prefers humus-rich soil and plenty of moisture. Plant so that its roots are shaded. It has a height and spread of 5 x 5 ft (1.5 x 1.5 m), eventually reaching 12 ft (3.5 m) in height.

### 7 *Actinidia kolomikta*
**Actinidia**

Grown for its foliage, this deciduous climber has long, heart-shaped leaves that appear to have been dipped in pink or cream. It needs full sun for good coloration. Its height is 10–13 ft (3–4 m).

### 8 *Humulus lupulus* 'Aureus'
**Golden Hop**

This rampant hop, which is festooned with typical hop flower bracts in fall, dies back each winter, when it should be cut back. It reaches a height of at least 13 ft (4 m) if grown in full sun.

### 9 *Ceanothus x delileanus* 'Gloire de Versailles'
## California Lilac

This wall shrub has sky-blue flowers from midsummer to early fall. Unlike some other species of ceanothus, which have flowers of varying shades of blue, it is not evergreen.

### 10 *Rosa* Iceberg
## Climbing Rose

This is a vigorous climbing rose, with double, white-flushed pink blooms that are sweetly scented, and glossy green foliage. It reaches 3 ft (1 m) in height.

### 11 *Ipomoea tricolor*
## Morning Glory

This annual climber can be grown through another, perennial climbing plant. It has good, clear royal-blue flowers, each bloom lasting only one day. It grows to 24 in (60 cm) high.

# Instant planting

"Instant" plants are those that have a rapid yearly growth and thus have an immediate impact on the area in which they are planted. All annuals come into this category, as do some biennials and fast-growing shrubs and climbers.

## Short-term impact

There can be gaps in even the most thoughtfully organized planting arrangements, and in such cases, annuals are indispensable. There are many other situations where annuals are useful, too. For example, many small urban spaces, such as roofs and windowsills, rely entirely on annuals as a source of color, particularly where conditions are too harsh for shrubs to overwinter. They are also useful for people who live in houses for short, seasonal periods and want a quick, colorful effect.

## Longer-term fillers

Annuals can also be of value to those who are trying to establish a long-term tree and shrub grouping, where fillers are needed to thicken out slower-growing material. For quick fill-ins at a lower level, use pot marigolds (*Calendula officinalis*) and forget-me-nots (*Myosotis* spp.). Evergreens take a particularly long time to establish; in this situation, fast-growing deciduous shrubs with a relatively short life span, such as broom (*Cytisus* spp..), can be used as long-term fillers and moved when appropriate.

Sunflowers (*Helianthus* spp.) and annual climbers, such as runner beans (*Phaseolus coccineus)*, hops (*Humulus lupulus*), and the cup-and-saucer vine (*Cobaea scandens*), are ideal for giving seasonal height to a maturing planting scheme or as a temporary screen while a hedging plant, such as boxwood or yew, grows.

## Biennials

Using biennials in the role of instant plants requires a little more advance planning, since they need to be planted one year to flower the next. Those that reach a considerable height include foxgloves (*Digitalis* spp.) and *Verbascum* spp.

## 1 *Tropaeolum majus*
### Nasturtium

The mixed hot colors of nasturtiums epitomize high
summer—Monet grew them across his path. They are very
easy to grow in a well-drained soil and can be trained
upward to reach 6½ ft (2 m). Alternatively, they can be left
to trail downward.

## 2 *Nicotiana x sanderae* Domino Series
### Tobacco Plant

These tobacco plants come in mixed colors or separately
in various colors, including this creamy white form. The
flowers release their scent in the evening, and the plants
have huge, tobacco-type, sticky green leaves. This useful
annual is 1 ft (30 cm) tall.

## 3 *Sambucus nigra*
### European Elder

Elders are invaluable for putting on up to 6½ ft (2 m) of
growth per season. These woody shrubs will grow anywhere
and come in a variety of shaped and colored leaves. They
should be used more often.

### 4 *Helianthus annus*
### Sunflower

I love sunflowers, which come in a range of shades, from white through yellow to orange and brown. Not all reach their top-end stature of 10 ft (3 m), the Mediterranean hybrids being half that height. They will thicken up a new shrub planting admirably. Grow these annuals in any soil in full sun.

### 5 *Cytisus x praecox*
### Broom

These fast-growing shrubs are ideal for creating a quick effect, but they are short-lived unless they are cut back after flowering. They therefore make good fillers. Grow in well-drained soil in a hot, sunny site.

### 6 *Calendula officinalis* 'Art Shades'
### Pot Marigold

Marigolds smell so good! Grown as annuals, once planted they are great self-seeders and keep coming back year after year. They grow to about 20 in (50 cm) in height.

## 7 *Passiflora caerulea*
### Passion Flower

This beautiful, vigorous climber has intriguing flowers 3–4 in (8–10 cm) wide, with white petals and a conspicuous ring of slender, purplish-blue filaments, followed by orange-colored, egg-shaped fruit. It grows by tendrils and prefers a spot against a warm wall.

## 8 *Matthiola incana* 'Giant Excelsior'
### Stock

Stocks are good biennial fillers, whose white, pink, or pale-blue flowers have a strong scent. Grow in any good soil, preferably in a sunny position. This variety reaches 2½ ft (75 cm) in height.

## 9 *Digitalis purpurea*
### Foxglove

Biennial foxgloves look superb in drifts in light shade. They shoot up very quickly, reaching about 3 ft (1 m). A white form is also available. They are persistent self-seeders.

# Planting for scent

There is nothing quite as alluring and luxurious as scent—something no small garden need ever be without, since many scented plants are climbers and thus take up little ground space, or can be planted in containers and enjoyed in any location. The smaller your space, the closer to your scented plants you will be, and the more enclosed it is, the more intense their fragrance.

Scented plants can be enjoyed outside, and from inside, through an open door or window. So why not get extra pleasure from them by planting roses around your bedroom window, aromatic herbs in a tub on your kitchen windowsill, or fragrant lilies in a container on your doorstep?

## Seasonal scents

Every season has its scents. Spring brings the fresh fragrance of hyacinths (*Hyacinthus orientalis*) and daffodils (*Narcissus* cvs.), both ideal for containers, followed by the sweet scent of *Wisteria* spp., *Clematis montana,* and lilac (*Syringa* spp.), which then mingles with the light, summer scents of roses and pinks (*Dianthus* spp.). These make way for the heady perfume of lilies (*Lilium auratum* and *L. regale* can be container-grown) and *Buddleja* spp. The exotic scents of jasmine (*Jasminum officinale*), gladioli (*Gladiolus* spp.), and tobacco plants (*Nicotiana* spp.) overlap with these and last into fall. During winter, we rely on the blossom of shrubs, such as sweet boxwood (*Sarcococca hookeriana* var. *humilis*) and *Daphne odora*, and the aromatic leaves of evergreen herbs, such as rosemary (*Rosmarinus officinalis*).

**Pet-friendly plants** (left) Pets, particularly cats, love the smell of herbs, with catnip or catmint (*Nepata* spp.), not surprisingly, being their favorite.

### 1 *Matthiola incana* Cinderella Series
**Stock**

Stocks, which are biennial, come in a lovely range of soft colors and also have a remarkable scent, which travels a significant distance. They are good either grown in pots and tubs or as fillers, preferably in sun. This is a dwarf form, about 10 in (25 cm) tall.

### 2 *Daphne mezereum*
**Daphne**

This is a small, rounded, evergreen shrub that bears soft purplish flowers with an extraordinarily sweet fragrance in early spring. Grow in a cool, moist, open position. Its height when mature is about 2 ft (60 cm), but it can eventually reach 4 ft (1.2 m).

### 3 *Rosmarinus officinalis*
**Rosemary**

This bushy evergreen herb has hooded blue flowers from midspring to early summer. Its fragrance comes from the oil in the dark green, needlelike leaves with white undersides. Grow in well-drained soil in a sunny position. It has a height and spread of 2½ x 2½ ft (75 x 75 cm), but can reach 5 ft (1.5 m) high over time.

### 4 *Cytisus battandieri*
**Moroccan Broom**

This broom has golden-yellow, pineapple-scented flowers from late spring to midsummer. Its foliage is covered with a silvery, satiny down. It is best grown against a warm wall. It has a height and spread of 10 x 6½ ft (3 x 2 m).

### 5 *Viburnum x carlcephalum*
**Viburnum**

There are many forms of fragrant viburnum. This one bears clusters of very fragrant white flowers in late spring. It also has good fall leaf color. It has a height and spread of 6½ x 5 ft (2 x 1.5 m).

### 6 *Salvia officinalis* 'Icterina'
**Sage**

This decorative sage has gray-green leaves variegated with gold. Plant in sun to ensure the typical sage-leaf fragrance. It prefers light soil. It has a height and spread of about 2 x 3 ft (60 cm x 1 m).

### 7 *Lavandula angustifolia*
**Old English Lavender**

Evergreen in mild climates and growing up to 2¾ x 2¾ ft (80 x 80 cm) in height and spread, lavender typically has pale grayish-blue flowers, appearing from late spring to late summer. Its fragrance comes from the oil in its silvery-gray foliage, which should be trimmed back with shears after flowering.

# Ground-cover planting

Ground-covering plants answer the call of awkward-shaped or "leftover" spaces, common in small, urban garden areas, that are difficult or even impossible to pave, or plant in a regular manner. They make an attractive, practical alternative to small areas of grass, which tend to look scruffy for much of the year and require a good deal of maintenance, and, provided the soil is cleared thoroughly before planting, make excellent weed suppressors.

### Link or contrast

Ground-cover plants can be used to link taller-growing plant groups within a small, mixed planting scheme, or on their own as a contrast to hard surfaces or areas of gravel. If you wish to confine your ground-cover planting to a particular area, do not choose plants described as rampant or invasive, since you will have difficulty keeping them under control; plants such as periwinkle (*Vinca major* and *minor*) fall into this category. Low-growing plants and taller, mound-forming plants can be used as ground cover. Among the former are perennials, such as *Ajuga* spp., which forms a dense mat of small leaves, *Bergenia* spp, which has large, eye-catching foliage, and the furry-leaved *Stachys lanata*. For year-round ground cover, choose an evergreen shrub, such as the low-growing *Cotoneaster dammeri*, or even consider a tall-growing evergreen that has dense ground-level growth, such as Mexican orange blossom (*Choisya ternata*).

"Ground-covering plants answer the call of awkward-shaped spaces"

### 1 Salix reticulata
**Willow**

This is a shrubby willow with prostrate stems that form a dense mat. It prefers a moist soil and will tolerate light shade. It has a height and spread of about 1½ x 8 in (4 x 20 cm).

### 2 Lamium maculatum 'Beacon Silver'
**Dead Nettle**

This is an ideal ground-covering plant for a cool soil that is partly shaded. Its leaves are entirely silvered, with green edging. It grows to a height of 4 in (10 cm).

### 3 Ceratostigma plumbaginoides
**Ceratostigma**

This is a plant for the fall garden. It forms creeping, colorful clumps of wiry stems, and its blue flowers look lovely against the crimson red of turning foliage. It is attractive to butterflies. It grows about 9 in (23 cm) high.

### 4 *Ceanothus thyrsiflorus* var. *repens*
**California Lilac**

A favorite from California, this low, evergreen shrub quickly forms a dense mound, which is covered in mid-blue flowers in late spring. It has a height and spread of about 1½ x 9 ft (45 cm x 2.7 m).

### 5 *Rosa* 'Hertfordshire'
**Ground-Cover Rose**

There is a range of ground-covering roses, varying in color and quality, known as the County Series. This variety has single carmine blooms and flowers profusely in sun. It has a height and spread of 2 x 4 ft (60 cm x 1.2 m).

### 6 *Heuchera micrantha* var. *diversifolia* 'Palace Purple' **Heuchera**

The range of heucheras gets larger and larger as leaf colors and markings are hybridized. This variety, however, has been around for some time and has a bronzy-red leaf surface with a pink underside. Its tiny, white, feathery flowers expand into rosy-bronze seed pods. It is a good plant to use en masse. It has a height and spread of 2 x 1 ft (60 x 30 cm).

### 7 *Geranium macrorrhizum* **Cranesbill**

The cranesbills are invaluable for their attractive, deeply cut leaves, vibrant flowers, and the weedproof ground cover they provide. The flowers are jewel-like in their intensity, ranging from white through pink and clear blue to this magenta, and are produced over a long period. They are easy to grow in ordinary soil and require a sunny site. They have a height and spread of about 1½ x 3 ft (45 x 90 cm).

### 8 *Vinca major* 'Variegata' **Greater Periwinkle**

This variegated form of periwinkle spreads by runners. A tough plant, it provides evergreen ground cover in shade, with lavender-blue flowers appearing in early spring. It has a height and spread of about 14 x 14 in (36 x 36 cm).

### 9 *Cotoneaster dammeri* **Cotoneaster**

There is a suitable cotoneaster for most situations. All have small white flowers in midsummer, followed by a huge crop of red or orange berries. A good evergreen ground cover, this species is quite prostrate and roots as it grows along, spreading indefinitely. It will hug a wall, growing downward. Its height is 2–3 in (5–7.5 cm).

# Plants for pots

Pots and containers really come into their own in the small-space garden, since they make it possible to grow plants of any size in any location. Also, they make it easy to move the plants around to create different arrangements throughout the year, and to change their location on impulse.

**Wall drama** (above) A fine *Yucca filamentosa* in a pot, making an impact against a contrasting-colored wall.

**Decorative duo** (opposite) *Verbena bonariensis* underplanted with the grass *Pennisetum villosum* or feathertop in a series of matching terra-cotta pots.

### Plant care

Just about any plants, ranging from small trees to vegetables and herbs, can be grown in a container, provided they are given adequate root space and are well watered and fed.

Drainage holes are essential to prevent the plant roots from rotting in the sour water that will collect at the bottom of a sealed container, and also because any collected water might freeze in winter, damaging the roots and, quite possibly, the container. Place a layer of porous material, such as pebbles or broken crockery, over the drainage holes.

The more potting mix you give a plant, the better (except for those that prefer poor soil), since the amount of moisture and nutrients retained will be greater. You should always give container-grown plants a good-quality mix—economizing on this will lead to disappointing results. To revitalize, replace the top layer of the mix each spring. Plants grown in exposed sites, or in hanging baskets, should be fed and watered even more regularly than those at ground level, since the potting mix is likely to be dehydrated by the wind. This is especially true of plants grown on balconies or in window-boxes.

### Special considerations

Terra-cotta containers dry out quickly, so soak them well before use and try lining their sides with plastic to aid moisture retention. Hanging baskets should be lined with plastic or a layer of moss. Pierce the plastic to allow stale water to drain out and the plants' roots to breathe.

"**move** containers and **pots** around to create different **arrangements**"

### 1 *Tulipa whittallii*
### Tulip

I am very fond of tulips in abundance. My particular favorites are the lily-flowered type, because they bend and swoop like swans' necks, particularly when used in containers. These grow to a height of 20 in–1 ft (50–60 cm).

### 2 *Sempervivum tectorum* 'El Toro'
### Houseleek

This is a mat-forming succulent with rosettes of bright red leaves. Other varieties of houseleek are mostly green-leaved and produce flowers in early and midsummer on tall stems. Grow in well-drained, gravelly potting mix, in flat stone sink containers, preferably in sun.

### 3 *Agapanthus* Headbourne Hybrids
### African Lily

The Headbourne hybrid agapanthus is more refined than the
larger *A. campanulatus*. It has closely set flower heads and
altogether grassier foliage. It comes in various blues and
whites, ranging in height from 20 in to 2½ ft (50–75 cm).

### 4 Zonal Pelargoniums
### Geranium

Good old geraniums—you can't beat them. They love hot,
dry conditions, when they flower continuously from early
summer to frost. In sheltered positions, they will survive
outside through the winter, or they can be lifted and stored
hung up indoors. However, they are just as easy to buy new,
from the huge range of flower colors and foliage interest
available. Alternatively, take cuttings.

# Plants for shade

Many small-garden spaces are overshadowed by tall buildings, walls, or overhanging trees. Some are cast in complete shade all the time; others get a short spell of sun as it describes its arc, before lapsing into shade again; and many are just shady in parts. The range of plants that will flourish in small, shady spaces (both damp and dry) is much wider than many people suspect, since often the very structures that cast the shade also give shelter.

Shade-loving plants frequently have large leaves (to enable them to photosynthesize). Their flowers tend to be muted in color, but in a confined space, any fragrance will hang heavy on the air. Areas of shaded planting can be highly atmospheric—lush foliage around a shaded water feature, perhaps, or pale flowers peeping out from a dark corner.

**Shade staples** (above) *Fatsia japonica* and *Hosta* spp. are stalwarts for temperate shade.

**Urban jungle** (opposite) In sheltered urban areas, you can go quite tropical.

## Shade-plant selection

Evergreen shrubs are invaluable shade "fillers." Shady urban spaces that are sheltered, frost-free, and fairly moist are perfect for camellias (*Camellia* spp.). Their smooth, gleaming foliage will give shady areas an attractive luster all year, and their cup-shaded flowers a vivid splash of seasonal color.

Among my favorite perennials are the strongly shaped *Bergenia cordifolia*, which has large leathery leaves, and *Iris foetidissima* and *Liriope muscari*, which I like for their spiky, evergreen foliage. Bamboos (*Arundinaria* spp.) will grow in any dry, sheltered, and shady spot. Their tall, vertical forms make an interesting contrast with the fronded, curved foliage of ferns. For a more delicate touch, plant Japanese anemones (*Anemone x hybrida*), which have dainty flowers and spreading growth. Lilies (*Lilium* spp.) can be grown in pots; they have exotic flower forms and will scent your shaded retreat.

If your shaded area is always moist—under the dripline of an established tree, for instance—plant the large-leaved *Rheum palmatum* and *Gunnera manicata* for an exotic, "tropical rain forest" effect. Other suitable shrubs for moist areas include hydrangeas, and *Viburnum davidii* and *V. rhytidophyllum*. *Hosta* spp. need plenty of moisture and are great shade survivors (if you can keep the snails at bay).

### 1 *Bergenia* 'Abendglut'
### Bergenia

In the depths of winter, thick flower stems start to rise from the huge, leathery foliage of this hardy perennial; by spring, they are covered with pink, bell-shaped blooms. Its foliage makes excellent shade ground cover. Both its height and spread range from 1 to 1½ ft (30–45 cm).

### 2 *Dicksonia antarctica*
### Tasmanian Tree Fern

I am trying to develop a taste for tree ferns, which still seem very alien to me. They are evergreen in a mild climate, though preferring a frost-free environment. They can reach up to 10–13 ft (3–4 m) in height.

### 3 *Mahonia aquifolium*
### Oregon Grape

This small, tough, evergreen shrub has bright-yellow, spring flowers and blue-black fall berries, and provides good ground cover in dry, shady sites. It is resilient enough to grow in exposed sites, such as balconies. It has a height and spread of 3 x 2 ft (1 m x 60 cm), eventually reaching 6 ft (1.8 m) in height.

### 4 *Polystichum setiferum*
### Soft Shield Fern

Ferns are indispensable shade-lovers, their fronded foliage
and arching form bringing atmospheric interest to all
manner of awkwardly shaped nooks and crannies. Most
useful are those that are evergreen, such as this species.
It has a height and spread of 4 x 3 ft (1.2 x 1 m).

### 5 *Convallaria majalis*
### Lily-of-the-valley

Lily-of-the-valley, a lover of moist, shady conditions, fills the
spring air with an exquisite fragrance. The foliage is simple
and neat, the flowers dainty. It grows to a height of 6–8 in
(15–30 cm).

### 6 *Helleborus argutifolius*
### Hellebore

I know this plant as *H. corsicus*, and it is a beauty. Early in the year, apple-green flower cups spring from handsome clawlike foliage of cool jade green—an architectural addition. It has a height and spread of 3 x 2 ft (1 m x 60 cm).

### 7 *Aucuba japonica* 'Salicifolia'
### Japanese Laurel

The gleaming green leaves and bright red berries of this form of *Aucuba japonica* will bring a breath of life to the driest and shadiest of corners (variegated forms such as *A. japonica* 'Variegata' do better in light shade). Being tolerant of atmospheric pollution, it is ideally suited to town and city gardens. It has a height and spread of 5 x 4 ft (1.5 x 1.2 m), ultimately reaching 10 ft (3 m) high.

### 8 *Liriope muscari*
### Lily Turf

This evergreen hardy perennial can be grown in containers and can thus be enjoyed in the smallest of shady sites; it also makes excellent ground cover. By early fall, the tall stems that rise from the elegant leaves are covered with tiny droplet-shaped flowers. It grows to 1 ft (30 cm) high.

9  10

### 9 *Euphorbia amygdaloides* var. *robbiae*
### Wood Spurge

This euphorbia grows well In dry shade, its rosettes of leaves forming a textured, evergreen mat, which is covered by yellow flowers in spring. It has a height and spread of 1½ x 1½ ft (45 x 45 cm).

### 10 *Anemone x hybrida* 'Honorine Jobert'
### Wind Flower

*Anemone x hybrida* is one of my personal favorites, since it has a simple flower shape, tall, elegant stems, and handsome foliage, and will grow in light shade. It is quite long-lived, but resents disturbance once it has become established. This variety has single, white flowers and grows to about 5 ft (1.5 m) in height.

# Plants for exposed places

Plants on roofs, balconies, and high window ledges are exposed to far greater extremes of heat, cold, and wind than those at ground level. The wind not only buffets plants, but dehydrates the soil in which they are grown—an effect intensified by the sun. However, there is a considerable range of plants that are able to survive such inhospitable conditions, and many others that can survive a season, or longer, if shelter is provided by a fence, canvas windbreak, or tough shrub, such as a form of juniper.

Plants grown in containers (as those grown above ground level are likely to be) have a limited nutrient and moisture reserve, so always use a nutrient-rich, moisture-retentive potting mix and water frequently.

**Tropical gem** (above) *Chamaerops*, the fan palm, can take heat and drought, but does not like too much wind or frost.

## Tough permanent planting

Tough, shrubby material can be used to give year-round interest, and to shelter your and your less-hardy plants from the wind. Look to those that are adapted to survive conditions on open ground, such as on heaths, mountainsides, or by the sea. All the brooms are tough (*Cytisus* spp., *Genista* spp., and *Spartium* spp.), as are the gorse family (*Ulex* spp.), various heaths and heathers, evergreen and "evergray" herbs, most conifers, and many grasses. Climbers in exposed locations are likely to take a considerable beating from the wind, so stick to deciduous ones (these are naturally tougher than evergreens), such as Virginia creeper (*Parthenocissus* spp.) and honeysuckle (*Lonicera* spp.). Alternatively, use resilient evergreen climbers like ivy (*Hedera* spp.).

## Plants for seasonal interest

Many plants will survive a season on a balcony, window ledge, or rooftop, particularly if they can be given shelter and are well cared for. Mass spring and summer bulbs and annuals in containers to add a flamboyant dash of seasonal color. Plants with a daisy flower are usually tough; these range from the smallest blue daisy (*Felicia* spp.), through to the exuberant yellow *Rudbeckia* spp., and a long-standing favorite, white *Leucanthemum x superbum*.

### 1 *Cytisus nigricans*
**Broom**

This erect, deciduous shrub, with yellow, broomlike flowers, can withstand tough conditions but prefers acidic soil. It has a height and spread of 3 x 3 ft (1 x 1 m), eventually expanding to 5 ft (1.5 m) in height.

### 2 *Hippophaë rhamnoides*
**Sea Buckthorn**

Wind-resistant and salt-tolerant, sea buckthorn makes a large shrub with character. It has silvery-white leaves and orange-red berries through the winter. Plant a male with one or two females to ensure pollination by wind. It has a height and spread of 6 x 10 ft (1.8 x 3 m), eventually reaching 13 ft (4 m) in height.

### 3 *Viburnum betulifolium*
**Viburnum**

All viburnums are easy to grow as well as tough. Many have sweetly scented flowers, while others have a good show of berries in fall.

### 4 *Santolina pinnata* ssp. *neopolitana* 'Sulphurea' **Santolina**

This dwarf evergreen shrub has delicate, silvery-gray foliage, with masses of sulfur-yellow flowers in mid- to late summer. It grows to a height of 1½ ft (45 cm).

### 5 *Olearia x haastii* **Daisy Bush**

This easily grown evergreen is wind-resistant and tolerant of any soil. It is also sun-loving. It forms huge mounds of white flowers from July onward. It has a height and spread of 4 x 4 ft (1.2 x 1.2 m).

### 6 *Spartium junceum* **Spanish Broom**

Almost leafless, rushlike stems carry large, honey-scented pea-shaped, bright-golden flowers all summer long. It will thrive in light soil and will reach a height of 8¼ ft (2.5 m).

### 7 *Lupinus arboreus*
**Tree Lupine**

This busy evergreen shrub grows quickly and vigorously, and bears pealike yellow flowers from early to late summer. It grows to a height of about 5 ft (1.5 m).

### 8 *Escallonia* 'Iveyi'
**Escallonia**

I find that many escallonias are straggly growers, but this variety has a strong, upright habit, with dark, glossy leaves and white flowers in August. It is an evergreen shrub, which grows to about 5 x 5 ft (1.5 x 1.5 m) in height and spread, but can eventually reach 9 ft (2.7 m) tall.

### 9 *Euphorbia polychroma*
**Spurge**

This is an interesting spot plant, producing a mass of brassy yellow flower heads throughout the spring. It becomes coral-colored in fall. It grows to a height of 15 in (40 cm).

# Country-style planting

Most people have an image of the country garden with full, billowing outlines, gentle colors, soft fragrances, and air of calm. Understandably, many yearn to capture these characteristics in their small-garden space, among apartment blocks and busy roads, and the general hurly-burly of urban life.

There are many plants that evoke the country-garden "feel," and some of my favorites are featured here. Such plants can be combined to create a tapestry of country planting in a small bedding scheme; or just one or two, planted in containers, can be used to give your doorstep, windowsill, or balcony a country-style look.

**Country mix** (right) An urban-crafted tapestry of color that is strongly reminiscent of a true country mix.

**Country coupling** (below) Climbing roses and foxgloves are two plants essential for creating the country look.

## Creating a country tapestry

Though at first glance the true country garden appears to be the result of relaxed, almost random planting, beneath the "flesh" lie "bones," in the form of paths, walls, arches, and other hard elements, plus bold, structural plantings, which prevent the informal planting scheme from becoming a jumbled mess. Even in a small town space, any bedding scheme of essentially nonarchitectural country planting, such as love-in-a-mist (*Nigella damascena*), lupines (*Lupinus* spp.), and delphiniums (*Delphinium* spp.), needs to be punctuated by permanent features such as a bench, a piece of sculpture, and/or plants with bold form, like the evergreen shrubs Mexican orange blossom (*Choisya ternata*), rosemary (*Rosmarinus officinalis*), and sage (*Salvia officinalis*). These will calm and steady your country tapestry

when annuals and perennials burst into flower, and give it shape and interest during the winter months.

One of the charms of the country garden is its fullness, which comes from plants smothering walls and overflowing from their beds. This look can be created in the smallest of spaces by allowing self-seeders to grow through gravel and between the cracks in paving, and by covering walls and fences with climbing plants.

Do not be tempted to give your urban "country garden" a sentimental overlay of "quaint" charm with "old-timey" artifacts, since this will immediately give it a contrived and self-conscious appearance. Rely instead on the colors, scents, and textures of your "country" plants and the style of indigenous features.

## 1 *Alchemilla mollis*
### Lady's Mantle

This is a fairly ubiquitous little plant, but extremely pretty all the same in both its leaves, which catch raindrops, and its frothy, yellowy-green flower heads that appear in early summer. It is a great self-seeder, with a height and spread of 20 x 30 in (50 x 75 cm).

## 2 *Rubus* 'Benenden'
### Rubus

Almost like a single rose, this close relative is easy to grow and bears its profusion of pure white flowers, with central golden stamens, all through the summer. It has a height and spread of 6½ x 6½ ft (2 x 2 m).

## 3 *Angelica archangelica*
### Angelica

This lovely plant is from the herb garden, with domed heads of cow-parsley-type flowers from early to late summer. It is a biennial and grows to about 6½ ft (2 m) in height.

## 4 *Fritillaria meleagris*
### Snake's-Head Fritillary

I have never found fritillaries easy to grow—they need fertile and well-drained soil. More for the meadow than the border, I would try to grow them in pots. The exceedingly beautiful and delicate, bell-shaped, mottled flowers of this form appear in spring. It grows to about 10 in (25 cm) high.

## 5 *Leucanthemum x superbum*
### Shasta Daisy

This is an indispensable hardy perennial for the cottage-style border, bearing its daisy flower heads throughout July and August. Grow in full sun. It has a height and spread of 3 x 2 ft (1 m x 60 cm).

## 6 *Eschscholzia californica*
### California Poppy

These are wonderful, mainly annual self-seeders—scatter them around and you will have them forever. Yellow and orange flowers are borne above feathery, blue-gray foliage from early summer to midfall, to give a very casual effect. The plant grows to a height of about 8 in (35 cm).

### 7 *Syringa villosa*
**Lilac**

This is an erect, branched shrub of compact habit. The lilac-rose flowers are held in stiff panicles in late spring. It is happy in most soils and full sun and grows to about 6–10 ft (1.8–3 m) high.

### 8 *Verbascum* 'Gainsborough'
**Mullein**

From a rosette of gray-green basal leaves grow tall branching spires of pale lemon-yellow flowers from June until later summer. This verbascum grows to about 4 ft (1.2 m) high.

### 9 *Nigella damascena*
**Love-in-a-mist**

This annual is a real old-fashioned favorite. Lovely, delicate, blue rosette flowers appear in early or midsummer amid a mist of feathery, green foliage. It has a height and spread of 20 x 10 in (50 x 25 cm).

### 10 *Achillea* 'Moonshine'
**Yarrow, Milfoil**

A good soil, sun, or shade will suit this silvery-foliaged perennial, which has clusters of sulfur-yellow, flat flower heads in summer and gray-green leaves. This hybrid variety grows to a height of about 2 ft (60 cm).

### 11 *Rosa* 'Constance Spry'
**Climbing Rose**

Climbing roses, where applicable, are a key part of the cottage-garden scene. The blooms of 'Constance Spry', borne along stems in midsummer, are richly myrrh-scented and an attractive clean pink. Grows up to about 6 ft (1.8 m) high.

### 12 *Echinops ritro*
**Globe Thistle**

The architectural shape of this plant make it perfect for the back of a border. The spiny, cobwebbed leaves provide interest from spring until the blooms appear in late summer. It grows to a height of about 2½ ft (75 cm).

10

11

12

# Plants with form

Architectural plants are the horticultural equivalent of exclamation marks and dramatic pauses. They have a strong overall form that comes from dramatic leaf, stem, or branch shape, and can be used in isolation to make a single bold statement or to give structural backbone to a mixed scheme of loosely formed planting.

"give structural **backbone** to a mixed scheme of **loosely** formed planting"

### Various effects

The effect of architectural plants varies according to their shape. The Italian cyprus (*Cupressus sempervirens* 'Stricta') has a slim, elegant form that makes an eye-catching outline against urban landscapes and open skylines; Irish yew (*Taxus baccata* 'Fastigiata') does the same in a more robust way. At the shrubby level, architectural plants include *Fatsia japonica* and *x Fatshedera lizei*. Both can be grown in containers and have flamboyant foliage that particularly suits urban locations. For a pleasing rounded outline, choose *Choisya ternata*, and for a spiky silhouette, opt for yuccas and phormiums. Perennials with architectural merit include the genus *Hosta* and *Bergenia cordifolia* cultivars. Planted in bold masses, they will punctuate and steady the fuzzy accumulation of other perennials, whose fleeting merit is their flowers. Climbers with strong leaf shape, such as the rather vigorous, ornamental vine *Vitis coignetiae*, and all the large-leaved *Hedera* genus, bring shape and pattern to all manner of vertical surfaces.

**Feature foliage** (left) Silver green *Astelia* leaves in the foreground, with *Phormium tenax* beyond.

### 1 Rhus typhina
### Staghorn Sumac

The cut-leaf staghorn sumac has a good craggy form. The antler-shaped branches are emphasized after leaf fall. It has a height and spread of 12 x 16 ft (3.5 x 5 m), although after many years it will eventually grow to 26 ft (8 m) tall.

### 2 Rodgersia podophylla
### Rodgersia

This perennial has enormous leaves, up to 1 ft (30 cm) in width, and spires of creamy flowers. It grows well in moist conditions and makes a good contrast with water plants with a vertical form, such as *Iris laevigata*. It has a height and spread of 3 x 4 ft (1 x 1.2 m).

### 3 Choisya ternata 'Sundance'
### Mexican Orange Blossom

The golden variety of this evergreen shrub has a gently rounded form that will give your garden space a pleasing, subtle rhythm year-round. In late spring, its glossy, golden foliage is offset by large clusters of fragrant white flowers. It can be planted in sun or light shade, but needs to be sheltered from sharp winds. It has a height and spread of 3 x 3 ft (1 x 1 m), eventually growing to 6 ft (2 m) high.

### 4 *Cordyline australis* Purpurea Group
**Cabbage Tree**

This tree has a strongly vertical form and long, sword-shaped leaves, which look especially striking against a plain backdrop. It has a height and spread of 8 x 6½ ft (2.4 x 2 m), eventually growing to 16 ft (5 m) high after many years.

### 5 *Juniperus scopulorum*
**Rocky Mountain Juniper**

As a substitute for the Italian cypress (*Cupressus sempervirens*), which gets too large for a small space, you might try this juniper, which is narrowly columnar and reaches no more than 8¼ ft (2.5 m).

### 6 *Phormium cookianum*
**New Zealand Flax**

This spectacular architectural plant has swordlike leaves. This form is slightly smaller than *P. tenax*, with 3-ft- (1-m-) high striped leaves, although it is not as tough.

### 7 *Taxus baccata* 'Fastigiata'
## Irish Yew

This native tree has a more robust, dark vertical emphasis than the juniper and is tolerant of most soils and situations. It grows to a height of 6½ ft (2 m); the golden form is slightly smaller. It can be clipped to form a shaped hedge.

### 8 *Allium hollandicum*
## Onion

This perennial bulb produces spherical, purplish-pink flowers in late spring, which, when grown en masse, are particularly striking. It grows to a height of 3 ft (1 m).

### 9 *Melianthus major*
## Honey Bush

The lovely blue-gray foliage of this shrub grows up to 10 ft (3 m) in height, but it can be cut back each winter. It bears strange brown-red flowers in late summer.

# Grasses

Grasses are comparative newcomers to the garden scene, although pampas grass (*Cortaderia* spp.) and gardener's garters (*Phalaris* sp.) were known in earlier, Edwardian gardens. Their use is not easy, and just dropping in the odd grass to an established herbaceous or mixed border to be fashionable does not work. Grasses are best seen en masse, sometimes mixed with other perennials.

## Growing conditions

The vogue for grasses originated jointly from Europe and from the prairies of North America. Both these locations have a continental climate of hot, dry summers and cold, snowy winters. Grasses grown in soil that has been amended or fertilized may have too soft a growth and be blown over in midsummer storms. Under the right conditions, though, grasses can look spectacular, especially in fall, when they associate with asters, sedums, and rudbeckia. However, they are probably only suitable for the largest of small gardens.

**Graceful grass** (left) *Stipa calamagrostis* has a dense growth habit and graceful, brushlike, silvery-white flower heads on arching stems.

### 1 *Cortaderia selloana*
### Pampas Grass

The well-known pampas grass has coarse tussocks, from which rise tall, elegant, silvery-white panicles in summer. It was once overused as a specimen plant, but new, more graceful varieties are now available and look especially effective when grown together. It has a height and spread of 3 x 3 ft (1 x 1 m).

### 2 *Arundo donax* var. *versicolor*
### Giant Reed

This 6-ft-high (2-m-) grass is probably best grown on its own, or it can be too large and overwhelming for a small space. The variegated form is less hardy than the species, but is quite spectacular.

### 3 *Pennisetum alopecuroides*
### Fountain Grass

This is a profusely flowering, clump-forming grass about 2–2¾ ft (60–80 cm) high. Its leaves spray outward and turn gold in fall. It bears red-brown flower spikes, like tiny foxtails, in late summer.

### 4 *Miscanthus sinensis* 'Silver Feather'
### Miscanthus

This columnar feature grass has ribbonlike leaves and tall stems that carry upright shuttlecocks of silver-beige plumes. It grows to 6 ft (2 m) in height.

### 5 *Stipa capillata*
### Feather Grass

Arching clumps of fine foliage bear long, trailing flower heads that are silvery-white but darken in fall. It requires a warm, sunny position and blooms in late summer. It grows to about 2 ft (60 cm) in height.

### 6 *Helictotrichon Sempervirens*
### Helictotrichon

This grass forms arching stems of bright, gray-blue foliage, with oatlike flower heads of the same color. Growing to about 4 ft (1.2 m), it is a useful plant at this height.

### 7 *Carex elata* 'Aurea'
### Golden Sedge

This bright, golden sedge bears clusters of brown flowers. It prefers a sunny position in damp soil. It would look good planted near water. It grows to 2 ft (60 cm) in height.

### 8 *Festuca valesiaca* var. *glaucantha*
### 'Silver Sea' Silver Fescue

This is the bluest of the blue grasses, and needs to be grown en masse for maximum effect. Contrast it with sempervivum, thyme, or dianthus. It needs full sun and dry soil. It grows to 9 in (23 cm) in height.

# Topiary and plants that can be clipped

Though topiary (the art of clipping plants to shape) brings to mind images of 17th-century country gardens, decorated with grand pyramids of yew and peacocks of boxwood, in a scaled-down form, it is just as relevant to small, urban spaces today. Topiary's neatly tailored shapes suit the strong lines and hard shapes of built environments.

### Topiary styles

Plants cut into contrasted shapes can be grouped together to make a dramatic display against a plain backdrop, such as a painted wall, or single plants used as individual points of emphasis in the overall design of a space. Simple, geometric shapes suit small spaces better than complex, figurative ones. Where topiary plants are adjacent to a building, why not echo the shape of architectural features (even a window shape) in your clipping?

In early 20th-century Scandinavian gardens, hedging plants were neatly clipped to give strong, linear definition, which contrasted with the natural, loose shapes of other plants. Following this tradition, but in a small space, you might clip a hedging plant, such as boxwood, to create a simple pattern, and contrast it with a plain background, such as a pale-colored gravel, or softer plant forms. Topiary plants always look most effective in simple containers (ornate ones will distract) and can be used to bring a theatrical flavor to the smallest of spaces, such as a doorstep or narrow passageway.

### Plant care

Many topiary plants are naturally greedy feeders, and their demands increase as they are clipped back and attempt to put out new shoots, so always use a rich potting mix, and feed and water them regularly. Place them in sunlight to encourage maximum growth and keep out of strong winds.

**Green sculpture** (left) This traditional peacock-shaped topiary is an impressive sight.

## 1 *Buxus sempervirens*
**Boxwood**

The deep green, glossy leaves of boxwood provide the perfect foil for flowering plants. Here, balls of boxwood line this bed of bergenia, which will eventually form a hedge. Boxwood can be grown freely as well as clipped.

## 2 *Ilex aquifolium*
**Holly**

Holly does not grow quickly, so once you have a topiary in holly, you do not need to clip it so often. By clipping holly, you remove the flowers that produce berries, but the variegation of some varieties has a strong enough impact alone.

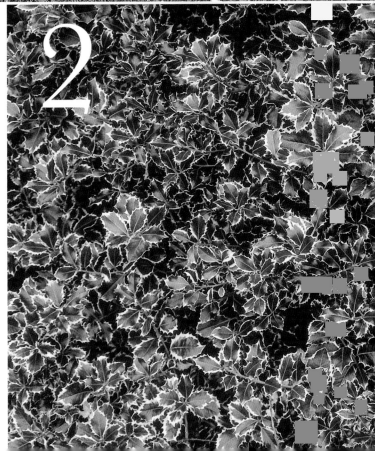

### 3 *Ilex crenata*
### Japanese Holly

This form of holly has tiny, glossy leaves and grows very slowly. It produces small, shiny, black fruits if not clipped too much, and is not used enough.

### 4 *Fagus sylvatica*
### Common Beech

Beech does make a handsome hedge, but can sometimes be too vigorous for a small garden. Although it is deciduous, it holds its leaves well in winter, to glow in the low sunlight.

### 5 *Crataegus monogyna*
### Common Hawthorn, May

Hawthorn is very tough and hardy, and makes a good hedge. It can also be clipped to great effect It will successfully grow almost anywhere.

## 6 *Pyracantha* spp.
### Firethorn

I am very fond of pyracantha for its tiny, white flowers in early summer, followed by long-lasting yellow, orange, or red berries from late summer to fall. It can form an attractive clipped lattice and convenient wall. Pyracanthas were once subject to fire blight, but newer varieties seem free of the problem.

## 7 *Carpinus betulus* 'Hornbeam'
### Common Hornbeam

Like beech, hornbeam hangs on to its deciduous leaves through winter. It has slightly denser vegetation than beech and is used extensively in Europe for clipping and topiary work.

## 8 *Ligustrum* spp.
### Privet

Something of a greedy feeder, impoverishing the ground around it, privet can nevertheless be easily clipped, and grows quickly as well.

# Plants for watery places

The smallest and most formal of water features can be enhanced by planting in the water and around it. Recreating the natural pond look (both in the style of a water feature and planting) in a small-space garden is not advisable, since this leads to a contrived and self-conscious appearance.

### Planting in water

The smaller the area of water, the more restrained both the number and the variety of plants should be. A strong effect can be created by simply planting one type of plant in a pool, or if you have a collection of water-filled barrels, a different type of water plant in each. The vertical stems and leaves of irises, sedges, and flags can be used as a dramatic contrast to the smooth surface of still water. Plants with floating leaves have a more restful appearance.

 If space allows, a combination of horizontal and vertical plant forms can be used. Marginal plants with vertical or arching forms make an effective visual counterbalance to a water jet or water pouring from a spout.

 Floating aquatics, such as water lilies, should be planted in plant baskets or pots. Marginal plants (which grow in shallow water) should be similarly planted and placed on a step at a suitable height in the water.

### Planting around water

Plants can be used to soften the division between a formal water feature and the rest of the garden, to extend the mood of any planting in a pool, and to make reflections in the water. Plants with lush foliage, such as hostas, ferns, and bamboos, are moisture-loving and naturally suit a waterside setting. If the area around your water feature is not naturally damp, grow them in containers, and water plentifully.

**Space invader** (right) The strong leaf shapes of water plants are tempting to use, but this large, round-leaved *Petasites japonicus* var. *giganteus* may be too invasive; yellow flag is much more manageable in a small garden.

### 1 *Alisma plantago-aquatica*
### Water Plantain

The long stalks of this shallow water plant hold its clumps of pointed green leaves well above the water line. Delicate flower stalks, which rise to a height of 2 ft (60 cm), and a mass of tiny, white flowers create a hazy summer background to the stronger shapes of the plantainlike leaves.

### 2 *Iris pseudacorus* CVS.
### Yellow Flag

This is a luxurious and vigorous beardless iris. *I. pseudacorus* var. *bastardii* is less rampant and has pale creamy yellow flowers. Heights vary, from the dwarf form at 2 ft (60 cm) to 6 ft (2 m).

### 3 *Nymphaea* 'Virginalis'
### Water Lily

The pure white, tapered petals of this water lily make a cool contrast with its dark green foliage. Although it is slow to establish, patience pays off, since it has one of the longest flowering seasons of any water lily, often lasting more than four months. A single plant can spread to a width of approximately 6 ft (2 m). It will grow in water up to 3 ft (90 cm) deep.

3

## 4 *Nymphaea* 'Escarboucle'
### Water Lily

The strident coloring of this water lily (deep red petals with deep yellow anthers, and dark green leaves) make it one that is best appreciated on its own, rather than in association with other aquatics. Plant in a medium-sized rather than small pool, since a single plant will spread to a width of approximately 6 ft (2 m). It will grow in water up to 1½ ft (45 cm) deep and once established will bear an abundance of blooms that last from summer through to early fall.

## 5 *Hydrocleys nymphoides*
### Water Poppy

For a refreshing composition, plant the yellow-flowered water poppy in a wooden tub (filled three-quarters full of soil and a quarter full of water).

## 6 *Acorus calamus* 'Variegatus'
### Sweet Flag

The spiky vertical form of this rush makes a clean contrast with the smooth, horizontal surface of still water. It is a marginal plant and grows in shallow water. It grows to about 3 ft (1 m) tall.

### 7 *Hosta lancifolia*
**Plantain Lily**

This hosta has shiny, dark green leaves and produces a long display of deep lilac flowers in late summer. Grow in a damp situation rather than a wet one.

### 8 *Lysichiton americanus*
**Yellow Skunk Cabbage**

The spathes of this impressive plant appear in early spring and unfurl to display amazingly beautiful yellow flowers, which are followed by huge, paddle-shaped green leaves. Plant in a sunny position in mud or shallow water. It has a height and spread of 4 x 5 ft (1.2 x 1.5 m).

### 9 *Caltha palustris*
**Marsh Marigold, Kingcup**

The marsh marigold produces its buttercup-like flowers early in the year. There is also both a white and a double form. It is suitable for larger rather than small damp areas, with a height and spread of up to 20 x 24 in (50 x 60 cm).

# Index

Page numbers in *italics* refer to captions/illustrations

# Acknowledgements

This is the first time that I have updated a book which I had written some time previously. New experiences, they say, are always rewarding—I found this one rather traumatic, for while I agree (happily) now with a lot of what I wrote then, there were other things which seemed terribly dated, and which I have deleted.

I would like to thank David Lamb first of all, who resurrected me, as it were; Andrew Milne and the team at the Bridgewater Book Company who revamped me, I would like to say, but in fact it is the look of the book which they have revamped so successfully for Dorling Kindersley. Lastly, thanks to my PA Claudia Murphy who reprocessed my new text and captions on her miracle computer, while all around...!

There are also lots of owners I would like to thank for their patronage of our particular art form—for so it is—as well as their designers. I hope all designers are credited, but inevitably some of them, and some of the photographers too, may fall through the net. I apologize now if this is the case.

For anyone interested in employing a garden designer, I direct them to the website of the Society of Garden Designers (http://www.sgd.org.uk).

# Picture and design credits

2–3 Marianne Majerus Photography: Designer: Alastair Howe Architects; 4 *left* The Garden Collection/Liz Eddison: Designer: Jack Merlo, Fleming's Nurseries, Australia, 4 *right* Steve Gunther: Designer: Judy Kameon, USA; 5 *left* Garden Exposures Photo Library: Designer: Fiona Lawrenson; 5 *right* John Glover; 7 John Brookes; 9 Steve Gunther: Designer: Judy Kameon, USA; 10 Spike Powell/elizabethwhiting.com; 11 Jerry Harpur: Designer: Steve Martino, USA; 12–13 Marianne Majerus Photography: Designer: Ruth Collier; 14 The Garden Collection/Liz Eddison: Designer: Jack Merlo, Fleming's Nurseries, Australia; 14–15 The Garden Collection/Liz Eddison: Designer: Kate Gould; 16 The Garden Collection/Gary Rogers:Designers: Monika Johannes & Malte Droege-Jung; 17 *below* Steve Gunther: Designer: Paul Robbins, USA, 17 *above* Red Cover.com/Andreas von Einsiedel; 18–19 Marianne Majerus Photography: Claire Mee Designs; 19 Garden Exposures Photo Library: Bakers Garden/Gerhardt Jenner; 20–21 Clive Nichols: Designer: Bob Swain, Seattle, USA; 22 Leigh Clapp: Designer: Darryl Mappin; 23 Red Cover.com/ Amanda Turner; 24 Clive Nichols: Designer: Charlotte Sanderson; 25 *left* Jerry Harpur: Designer: Fergus Garret, 25 *right* Red Cover.com/ Polly Farquharson; 26–35 John Brookes; 37 Marion Brenner: Designer: Anni Jensen, California, USA; 38–39 Steve Wooster: Designer: Ben McMaster; 40–41 Steve Wooster: Designer: Luciano Giubbilei; 42 Steve Wooster: Designer: Di Firth, New Zealand; 43 *above* The Garden Collection/Liz Eddison: Designer: Marney Hall, 43 *below* Garden Exposures Photo Library: Victoria Kerr, Wilts; 44–45 Modeste Herwig: Designer: Jos V.D.Lindeloof ; 46 Red Cover.com/N Minh & J Wass; 47 John Brookes; 48 Marion Brenner: Designer: Stephen Suzman, California, USA; 49 Gil Hanly: Designer: Sophie Henderson, Haumoana, Hawkes Bay, New Zealand; 50 *above* Marion Brenner: Von Hellens, 50 *below* Nicola Browne: Designer: Ted Smyth, New Zealand; 51 *above* Nicola Browne: Designer: Ted Smyth, New Zealand, 51 *below* Clive Nichols: Designers: Alison Wear and Miranda Melville; 52–53 Gil Hanly: Designer: Ben McMaster, New Zealand; 54–55 DK Images/Steve Wooster; 55 *left* Colin Walton: www.marniemoyle.co.uk, 55 *right* The Garden Collection/Marie O'Hara; 56 Di Lewis/elizabethwhiting.com; 57 *left* Nicola Stocken Tomkins: West Green House Cottage, Hants, 57 *right* Clive Nichols: Designer: Sarah Layton; 58 Nicola Browne: Designer: Kristof Swinnen; 59 Arcaid.co.uk/Richard Powers/ Daniel Marshall Architect, New Zealand; 60 Derek St Romaine: Designer: Alistair Davidson; 61 Garden Exposures Photo Library: Design: The Plant Room; 62–63 John Brookes; 64 Marianne Majerus Photography: Designer: Marie Clarke; 65 Marianne Majerus Photography; 66 *below* Leigh Clapp: Owner: Johnathan Sunley/Designer: Jamie Higham, Greendot Gardens, 66 *above* Marianne Majerus Photography: Designer: George Carter; 67 *above* John Brookes, 67 *below* Nicola Stocken Tomkins: Designers: Capstick/Saddington/ Tatton Park Flower Show 2004; 69 *above* & *below right* John Brookes, 69 *above* & *below left* Colin Walton: Designer: John Brookes; 70–73 Colin Walton: Designer: John Brookes; 74–75 Brian T. North: Designer: John Brookes; 77 John Brookes; 78–79 Brian T. North: Designer: John Brookes; 80–83 Colin Walton: Designer: John Brookes; 84–85 DK Images/Geoff Dann; 85 John Brookes; 86 89 DK Images/Geoff Dann; 91 Clive Nichols: Designer: Joe Swift & Thamasin Marsh; 92–93 Garden Exposures Photo Library: Designer: Joe Swift for Sue Dubois;. 94 Jerry Harpur: Designer: Christoph Swinnen, Belgium; 95 Steve Wooster: Designer: Nigel Cameron; 96 *below* left & *right* John Brookes, 96 *above right* Philip Kerridge of Landscape Definitions; 98–101 Philip Kerridge of Landscape Definitions; 102–105 John Brookes; 106 *above left* Leigh Clapp, 106 *below left* Leigh Clapp: Designer: Peter Fudge, Gardening Australia Live, 106 *below right* Garden Exposures Photo Library: Design: Van Sweden Design, Washington DC, 106 *above right* Red Cover.com/Hugh Palmer; 107 Nicola Browne: Designer: Steve Martino, USA; 108 Leigh Clapp: 109 *above* Colin Walton, 109 *below* Anne Green–Armytage: Kent Design; 110 The Garden Collection/Liz Eddison: Designer: Bob Purnell 110–111 Colin Walton; 111 *below left* Colin Walton, 111 *right* The Garden Collection/Liz Eddison: Designer: David MacQueen, Orangenbleu; 112 *left* Nicola Browne: Designer: Trudy Crerar, 112 *right* Andrew Lawson: Designer: John Brookes, Altamont; 113 Nicola Browne: Designer: Ross Palmer; 114 *right* Henk Dijkman: Designer: Martien Koelemeijer, 114 *left* Jerry Harpur: Designer: Roberto Silva for Amanda Foster, Putney;

115 Garden Exposures Photo Library: Designer: Joe Swift for Sue Dubois. 116–117 www.helenfickling.com: Designer: Amir Schlezinger, Mylandscapes, London, 117 Henk Dijkman: Designer: Haneghem bv.; 118 John Glover: Designer: Allison Armour Wilson; 119 John Glover: Designer: Fiona Lawrenson, Chelsea Flower Show 1997/Artist: John Simpson.; 120 below DK Images/Steve Wooster: Designer: Jack Merlo, Fleming's Nurseries, Australia, 120 above The Garden Collection/Liz Eddison: Designer: Christopher Bradley-Hole, Chelsea Flower Show 2005; 121 left Arcaid.co.uk/Alan Weintraub: Designer: Isay Weinfeld, Brazil, 121 right Leigh Clapp: Designer: Peter Fudge/Gardening Australia Live; 122 The Garden Collection/Jonathan Buckley:Designer: Jackie McLaren, Westwood Park, London; 123 below Andrew Lawson, 123 above Derek St Romaine: Designers: Rob Jones, Mathew Stewart and Ben Gluszkowski, Tatton Park 2003; 124 below right Arcaid.co.uk/Alan Weintraub/Nathaniel and Margaret Owings, USA, 124 below left Marion Brenner: Design: Andrea Cochrane Landscape Architecture, California, USA, 124 above left Clive Nichols: Designers: Patrick Wynniat-Husey and Patrick Clarke, 124 above right View Pictures/Philip Bier; 125 right Nicola Browne: Designer: Ross Palmer, 125 left Bruce Hemming/elizabethwhiting.com; 126 Clive Nichols: Designer: Stephen Woodhams; 127 above Andrew Lawson: Designer: Anthony Noel, 127 below Marianne Majerus Photography; 129 Marianne Majerus Photography: Designer: George Carter; 130 Derek St Romaine: Designer: Andrew Anderson; 131 Sunniva Harte; 132 right John Glover: Sharon Osmund, Berkeley, California, 132 left Jerry Harpur: Bertholt Vogt, London; 133 Jerry Harpur: Designer: Philip Roche for Arlene Mann; 134 left Leigh Clapp: Taylor Cullity Design, 134 right View Pictures/Philip Bier; 136 Colin Walton, 136–137 Jerry Harpur: Designer: Christina Lemehaute, Buenos Aires, 137 Jerry Harpur: Designer: Christopher Masson; 138 above Nicola Browne: Designer: James van Sweden, USA, 138 below left Clive Nichols: Designer: Sarah Layton, 138 below right Clive Nichols: Designers: Bill Smith and Dennis Schrader, Long Island, USA; 140 Marianne Majerus Photography: Designer: Paul Gazerwitz; 140–141 Steve Wooster: Designer: Luciano Giubbilei; 142 John Glover: 143 left www.helenfickling.com: Designer: Amir Schlezinger, Mylandscapes, London, 143 right Marianne Majerus Photography: Designer: Susanne Blair; 144 above Nicola Browne: Designer: Ross Palmer, 144 below Marianne Majerus Photography: Designer: Christopher Bradley-Hole; 146 left John Glover: Designer: Steven Crisp, 146 right Andrew Lawson: Designer: Camilla Shivarg; 147 left Arcaid.co.uk/ Nicholas Kane/Sakula Ash Architects, 147 right Nicola Browne: Designer: Kim Wilkie; 148 right John Glover: Designer: Susy Smith, 148 left View Pictures/Paul Raftery; 150 Garden Exposures Photo Library; 151 above left & right John Glover, 151 below left Jerry Harpur: Designer: Annie Fisher, USA, 151 below right John Glover: Designer: Andrea Parsons, Chelsea Flower Show 1997; 152 John Glover; 153 Marianne Majerus Photography: Designer: Jill Billington; 154 The Garden Collection/Gary Rogers: Designers: Monika Johannes and Malte Droege-Jung; 155 above The Garden Collection/Liz Eddison: Designer: Kay Yamada,

155 center Marianne Majerus Photography: Designer: Natalie Charles, Merrist Wood, Chelsea Flower Show 2002, 155 below Modeste Herwig: Designer: Buro Vis a Vis; 157 Garden Exposures Photo Library: Designer: Fiona Lawrenson; 158–159 Derek St Romaine: Designer: Philip Nash; 159 www.helenfickling.com: Designer: Amir Schlezinger, Mylandscapes, London; 160 Colin Walton; 160–161 Steve Wooster: Designer: Nigel Cameron, New Zealand, 161 Colin Walton: Design: wrightgardens.co.uk; 162 above right Colin Walton, 162 above left www.helenfickling.com: Designer: Andrew Duff, Chelsea Flower Show 2004, 162 below left Anne Green-Armytage: Shirley Gilbert, Norfolk, 162 Derek St Romaine; 163 Jerry Harpur: Designer: Graham McCleary of Natural Habitat for Pierre and Sue Legrange, New Zealand; 164 Marianne Majerus Photography: The Surprise Gardeners, Chelsea Flower Show 2002; 165 Jerry Harpur: Designer: Topher Delaney, California, USA; 166 below Arcaid.co.uk/Richard Bryant, 166 above Steve Wooster: Designer: Ted Smyth. Architect: Ron Sang. New Zealand; 167 above Colin Walton, 167 below Jerry Harpur: Designer: Jenny Jones; 169 above right Arcaid.co.uk/George Seper: BELLE/Stephan and Simon Rodrigues, Australia, 169 below right Colin Walton, 169 below left www.helenfickling.com: Designer: Raymond Jungles, Inc, The Keys, Florida , 169 above left Garden Exposures Photo Library; 170 above Colin Walton, 170 center The Garden Collection/Liz Eddison; 170 below Maurice Nimmo/Frank Lane Picture Agency/CORBIS; 171 above left The Garden Collection/Liz Eddison: Designer: Jane Mooney, Hampton Court Flower Show 2002, 171 above center, The Garden Collection/Michelle Garrett, 171 above right The Garden Collection/Liz Eddison: Designer: Jill Brindle, Tatton Park Flower Show 2005, 171 center left The Garden Collection/Liz Eddison: Designer: Hannah Genders, Chelsea Flower Show 2004, 171 below left The Garden Collection/Gary Rogers, 171 below right The Garden Collection/Liz Eddison: Designer: Ali Ward; 172 Clive Nichols: Designers: Clive and Jane Nichols; 173 Derek St Romaine: Designer: Andrew Yates. 'Out of the Woods', Tatton Park Flower Show 2003; 174 left Colin Walton: Thanks to Doreen Armstrong, designed by Olive Gillespie, 174 right Marianne Majerus Photography: Claire Mee Designs; 175 above Leigh Clapp: Designer: Allison Armour-Wilson, 175 below The Garden Collection/Jonathan Buckley: Designer: Paul Kelly, Church Lane, London; 176 above Steve Wooster: Design: The Living Earth Company, Ellerslie Flowe Show 1998, New Zealand, 176 center Leigh Clapp: Design: Greendot Garden, 176 below John Brookes; 177 Nicola Browne: Designer: Ross Palmer. 178 above & center Colin Walton, 178 below Jefferson Smith for Gardenlife Magazine; 179 Jefferson Smith for Gardenlife Magazine; 180 Jerry Harpur: Designer: Kan Izue, Japan; 181 Gil Hanly: Designer: Chris Gloom; 182 above www.helenfickling.com: Designer: Catherine Mason, 182 below Leigh Clapp: Cherry Mills Garden Design; 183 left Marion Brenner: Designer: Bob Clark, California, USA, 183 right Gil Hanly: Julie Nicholson, Auckland, New Zealand; 184 Steve Wooster; 185 Garden Exposures Photo Library; 186–187 Anne Green-Armytage: Shirley Gilbert, Norfolk, 187 Nicola Browne: Designer: Isabelle Greene; 188 left The Garden Collection/Liz Eddison, 188 right Clive Nichols:

Designers: Joe Swift & Thamasin Marsh; **189** John Brookes; **190** *above* **Modeste Herwig:** Design: Landvast, Floriade 2002, **190** *center* Arcaid.co.uk/David Churchill/ Architects: Sticklandcoombe.com, **190** *below* **Clive Nichols:** Designers: Joe Swift & Thamasin Marsh; **191 Modeste Herwig:** Designer: Jan v.d.Kloet for Frenkel Frank; **192** *above left* **Andrew Lawson,** 192 *below left* **Nicola Browne:** Designer: Trudy Crerar, **192** *above right* **Colin Walton:** Designer: John Elliott, 192 *below right* John Glover: Designer: Karen Maskell, Hampton Court Flower Show 2000; **193** *left* **Andrew Lawson:** Designers: Kim Jarrett and Trish Waugh, Chelsea Flower Show 2004, **193** *right* Karl-Dietrich Buhler/elizabethwhiting.com; **194** *left* **Andrew Lawson:** Designer: Ryl Nowell, Wilderness Farm, **194** *right* John Glover: Designer: Maggie Howarth. Chelsea Flower Show 2004; **195** John Glover: Designer: Barbara Hunt; **197** *above left* **Garden Exposures Photo Library:** Designer: Sam Woodroofe, Modular Gardens, **197** *above right* **Garden Exposures Photo Library,** **197** *below left* **John Glover:** Fair Oaks, California, 197 *below right* **John Glover:** Designer: Huw Cox, Hampton Court Flower Show 2003; **198** *above* **David Lamb,** 198 *center* **John Brookes,** **198** *below* **Marianne Majerus Photography:** Designer: Bunny Guinness; **199** *above left* **David Lamb,** 199 *above center* **Nicola Browne:** Designer: LUT. British Embassy, Washington , **199** *above right* **Sunniva Harte,** 199 *center right* **Clive Nichols:** Designer: Alison Wear Associates, **199** *below right* **Nicola Browne:** Designer: Ulf Nordfjell, **199** *below left* **Derek St Romaine:** Designer: Cleve West; **200 Clive Nichols:** Designer: Tony Heywood, Conceptual Gardens, 'The Drop'; **201** **The Garden Collection**/Liz Eddison: Designer: Jackie Knight; **202** *above* **Garden Exposures Photo Library:** Designer: Joe Swift, The Plant Room, **202** *below left* **The Garden Collection**/Gary Rogers: Designers: Monika Johannes and Malte Droege-Jung, **202** *below right* **John Glover;** **203** *above left* Rodney Hyett/ elizabethwhiting.com, **203** *above right* **Marianne Majerus Photography:** Designer: Peter Chan, **203** *below* **Marianne Majerus: Design:** Gardens and Beyond; **204** *above* **Clive Nichols:** Design: Blakedown Landscapes, **204** *below* **Andrew Lawson:** Design: Courseworks, Mitsubishi, Hampton Court Flower Show 2001; **206** *above* www.helenfickling.com, **206** *center* **Nicola Browne,** 206 *below* **The Garden Collection/** Jonathan Buckley: Designer: Paul Kelly; **207** *above left* **Nicola Browne:** Designer: Isabelle Greene, **207** *above* right, *below* left & *below* center **Colin Walton,** 207 *center left* **The Garden Collection**/Marie O'Hara, **207** *below right* **The Garden Collection**/Liz Eddison; **208** Arcaid.co.uk/Alan Weintraub/John Lautner, USA; **209** *left* www.helenfickling.com: Designer: Amir Schlezinger, Mylandscapes, London, **209** *right* **Leigh Clapp:** Kingcups Garden; **211** *above left* **Colin Walton,** 211 *above right* **The Garden Collection**/Jonathan Buckley: Designer: Diarmuid Gavin, **211** *below* **John Glover:** Designers: Grant and Tatlock, Hampton Court Flower Show; **212** *above* **Nicola Browne:** Designer: Ross Palmer, **212** *below left* **Marianne Majerus Photography:** Design: Gardens and Beyond, **212** *below right* **Marion Brenner:** Design: Andrea Cochrane Landscape Architects, California, USA; **213 Sunniva Harte;** 214 **Modeste Herwig:** Design: Duotuin;

**215** *left* **The Garden Collection/**Liz Eddison: Designer: Michelle Brown, **215** *right* **Marion Brenner;** 216 **Clive Nichols:** Designer: Peter Reid, Hampshire; **217** *left* **Nicola Browne:** Designer: Ted Smyth, New Zealand, **217** *right* **The Garden Collection/**Liz Eddison: Designers: Katie Hines and Steve Day; **218** *left* **Garden Exposures Photo Library:** Keukenhof Gardens, The Netherlands, **218** *right* **John Glover:** Designer: Guy Farthing, Hampton Court Flower Show 2002; **219** *left* **The Garden Collection/**Liz Eddison: Folia Garden Designers. **219** *right* **Garden Exposures Photo Library;** 220 **Henk Dijkman:** Designer: Haneghem bv.; **221 Leigh Clapp:** Designer: Philip Nash; **222** *above* **Garden Exposures Photo Library,** **222** *below* **Steve Wooster;** 223 **The Garden Collection/**Gary Rogers: Designers: Monika Johannes and Malte Droege-Jung; **224** *above* left & *right* **Colin Walton,** 224 *below left* **The Garden Collection/**Liz Eddison/Designer: David MacQueen, Orangenbleu, **224** *below right* **Clive Nichols:** Designer: Amir Schlezinger, Mylandscapes, London; **225** *left* **Clive Nichols:** Designer: Charlotte Sanderson, **225 John Brookes;** 226 *left* **The Garden Collection/** Marie O'Hara, **226** *right* **John Glover:** Designer: Stephen Woodhams, Chelsea Flower Show 1997; **227** *left* **Garden Exposures Photo Library:** Heronswood, **227** *right* **John Glover:** Designer: Stephen Woodhams, Chelsea Flower Show 1997; **229 Marianne Majerus Photography:** Designer: Susanne Blair; **230 Colin Walton: 231** *above left* **John Glover:** Design: Landart. Hampton Court Flower Show 2000, **231** *above right* **Derek St Romaine,** 231 *below left* **Leigh Clapp:** Designer: Anthony Tuite, **231** *below right* **John Glover:** Designer: J Baille; **232** *above* **Leigh Clapp:** Designer: Jill Fenwick,, **232** *below* **The Garden Collection/** Derek Harris; **233 Colin Walton:** Designer: Ryl Nowell, Cabbages and Kings; **234** *above left* **John Glover:** Artist: Marion Smith, **234** *above right* **Derek St Romaine:** Designer: Liz Robinson, Hampton Court Flower Show 2003. 'The Garden of Words', **234 Clive Nichols:** Artist: Pat Volk/Hannah Pescher Gallery, Surrey; **235 Clive Nichols:** Designer: David Harber; **236 The Garden Collection/**Liz Eddison; **237 Marianne Majerus Photography:** Designer: Julie Toll; **238 Marianne Majerus Photography:** Claire Mee Designs; **239** *left* **Garden Exposures Photo Library:** Gennets, Napa Valley, California, **239** *above center* **Nicola Stocken Tomkins:** Designers: T Dann and S Beadle, Chelsea Flower Show 2004, **239** *above right* **The Garden Collection/**Liz Eddison: Designer: Julie Zeldin, **239** *below* center **Garden Exposures Photo Library:** Thompson Brookes, **239** *below right* **Leigh Clapp;** 240 Di Lewis/ elizabethwhiting.com; **241 Clive Nichols:** Designer: Peter Reid, Hampshire; **242** *left* Michael Dunne/ elizabethwhiting.com; **242** *right* **Steve Wooster:** Liz Morrow; **243** *left* **Jerry Harpur:** Designer: Steve Martino, Phoenix, USA, **243** *right* **Marianne Majerus Photography;** 244 **Marion Brenner:** Bernard Trainor Design Associates, California, USA; **245** *above & center* www.garpa.co.uk +44 (0) 1580 201 190, **245** *below* Photolibrary.com/Marion Brenner; **246** www.garpa.co.uk; **247** *above* **Nicola Browne:** Designer: Kim Wilkie, **247** *below* www.garpa.co.uk; **248** www.garpa.co.uk; **249** *above & below right* www.garpa.co.uk; **249** *below left* **Colin Walton; 250** *left* **Clive Nichols:** Designers: Joe Swift & Thamasin Marsh, **250** *right*

Andrew Lawson: Designer: Dan Pearson; 251 Marianne Majerus Photography: Designer: Paul Cooper; 252 The Garden Collection/Liz Eddison: Designer: Shirley Roberts; 253 above Clive Nichols: Design: Alison Wear Associates, 253 below left Modeste Herwig: Design: Buro Vis a Vis, 253 below right Derek St Romaine: Designer: Philip Nash/ Robert van den Hurk; 255 Marianne Majerus Photography: Designer: Sally Brampton; 256 Garden Exposures Photo Library: Designer: James Hitchmaugh, Sheffield; 257 Derek St Romaine: 258–259 Anne Green-Armytage; 261 Sunniva Harte: Designer: Michele Barker; 262 above Nicola Browne: Designer: Kristof Swinnen, 262 below Leigh Clapp: Merriments Garden; 263 John Glover: Designer: Fiona Lawrenson; 264 DK Images/Roger Smith; 265 above DK Images/Roger Smith, 265 below left DK Images/Andrew Lawson, 265 below right DK Images/Eric Crichton; 266 above left DK Images, 266 above right DK Images/Eric Crichton, 266 below left DK Images/Steve Wooster, 266 below right DK Images/Anne Hyde; 267 above DK Images/Andrew Lawson , 267 below DK Images; 268 DK Images: 269 left DK Images/James Young, 269 right DK Images/Andrew Lawson; 270 above DK Images, 270 below DK Images/Roger Smith; 271 left DK Images/Roger Smith, 271 right DK Images/Juliette Wade; 272 left DK Images/Jonathan Buckley, 272 right DK Images/Eric Crichton; 273 DK Images; 274 left DK Images/Roger Smith, 274 above right DK Images/Eric Crichton, 274–275 below DK Images/Steve Wooster; 275 above DK Images/Deni Bown, 275 below right DK Images/John Glover below right. 276 above DK Images/Andrew Henley, 276–277 below DK Images/Roger Smith; 277 DK Images/Roger Smith; 278 left DK Images/Roger Smith, 278 right DK Images/Andrew Lawson ; 279 DK Images; 280 DK Images/James Young; 281 left DK Images/John Glover, 281 right DK Images; 282 left DK Images/Roger Smith, 282 right DK Images/Howard Rice 283 left DK Images, 283 right DK Images/Roger Smith; 284 left DK Images/Roger Smith, 284 right DK Images/Andrew Butler; 285 DK Images/Andrew Lawson; 286 above DK Images/Roger Smith, 286 below DK Images; 287 above DK Images/Roger Smith, 287 below DK Images/Andrew Lawson; 288 Marianne Majerus Photography: Designer: Brita von Schoenaich. Chelsea Flower Show 2000; 289–290 DK Images; 291 above DK Images/James Young, 291 below DK Images; 292 Clive Nichols: Laurent-Perrier Harpers & Queen Garden, Chelsea Flower Show 2001; 293 above DK Images/ Neil Fletcher, 293 below left DK Images, 293 below right DK Images/Colin Walton; 294 DK Images/Roger Smith, 294 below left DK Images, 294 below right DK Images/ Howard Rice; 295 above DK Images/Andrew de Lory, 295 below left DK Images, 295 below right DK Images/Sarah Cuttle; 296 Janet Johnson; 297above DK Images/Howard Rice, 297 below left DK Images, 297 below right DK Images/Sarah Cuttle; 298 above & below left DK Images, 298 below right DK Images/Eric Crichton ; 299 DK Images/Neil Fletcher.; 300 John Glover: Designers: Smith and Alder, Hampton Court Flower Show 2004; 301 above left DK Images, 301 above right DK Images, Jerry Harpur, 301 below left DK Images/Roger Smith; 302 above

DK Images/James Young, 302 below DK Images; 303 above left DK Images, 303 above right DK Images/Andrew Lawson, 303 below left DK Images/Howard Rice, 303 below right DK Images/Peter Anderson; 304 Jerry Harpur: Cloudehill, Olinda, Victoria, Australia; 305 www.helenfickling.com: Designer: Amir Schlezinger, Mylandscapes, London; 306 DK Images; 307 above DK Images/Roger Smith, 307 below Garden Picture Library/ NouN; 308 John Glover: Chelsea Flower Show 1991. Daily Express; 309 Jerry Harpur: Designer: Peter Nixon, Paradisus Design, Sydney, Australia; 310 above DK Images/Roger Smith, 310 below DK Images, 310–311 Nicola Browne: Designer: Ross Palmer; 311 below left DK Images/Roger Smith, 311 below right DK Images/Eric Crichton, 312–313 DK Images; 314 Derek St Romaine: Designer: Philip Nash for Robert van den Hurkp; 315 above left DK Images/Eric Crichton, 315 above right DK Images, 315 below DK Images/Peter Anderson; 316 above DK Images/ Clive Boursnell, 316 below DK Images, 316–317 DK Images; 318 Marianne Majerus Photography; 319 Andrew Lawson: Designer: Dipika Price; 320 DK Images; 321 above & below left DK Images, 321 above right DK Images/John Glover, 321 below right DK Images/Eric Crichton; 322 above left DK Images/James Young, 322 above right DK Images/Beth Chatto, 322 below DK Images; 323 above DK Images/James Young, 323 below DK Images; 324 Jerry Harpur: Designer: James Fraser for Biddy Bunzle; 325 above left DK Images, 325 Marianne Majerus Photography: 325 below Garden World Images; 326 above left DK Images/James Young, 326 above right The Garden Collection/Marie O'Hara, 326 below DK Images/Colin Walton; 327 above left Garden Picture Library/Marijke Heuff 327 above right DK Images, 327 below DK Images/Roger Smith; 328 Steve Wooster: Designer: Gordon Collier; 329 left DK Images/Roger Smith, 329 right DK Images; 330 left DK Images/John Fielding, 330 above DK Images/Howard Rice, 330 below right DK Images/John Glover; 331 above & below left DK Images/Howard Rice, 331 below right DK Images/James Young; 332 Garden Picture Library: Janet Seaton/Designer: Charles Carey; 333 above DK Images, 333 below DK Images/Colin Walton; 334 above left DK Images, 334 above right Garden World Images, 334 below DK Images/Deni Bown; 335 above John Glover, 335 below left The Garden Collection: Liz Eddison: Designer: Chris Beardshaw, Hampton Court Flower Show 2004, 335 below right Garden Picture Library/Clive Nichols; 336–337 Garden Picture Library/Ron Sutherland; 338–339 DK Images; 340 DK Images; 341 above DK Images, 341 below left DK Images/Beth Chatto, 341 below right DK Images/Eric Crichton.